THE BEST OF TOMBSTONE HUMOUR

RICHARD DE'ATH

Foreword by
Spike Milligan

JAVELIN BOOKS
LONDON · NEW YORK · SYDNEY

This Javelin Books edition first published 1987
Javelin Books, Artillery House, Artillery Row,
London SW1P 1RT

First published in the UK 1983, 84, 85 and 86 by Unwin
Paperbacks

Reprinted 1987

Copyright © 1987 Javelin Books.

Distributed in the United States by
Sterling Publishing Co., Inc.,
2 Park Avenue, New York, NY 10016

Distributed in Australia by
Capricorn Link (Australia) Pty Ltd.
PO Box 665, Lane Cove, NSW 2066

British Library Cataloguing in Publication Data

The Best of Tombstone humour
  1. Epitaphs   2. English wit and humor
I. De'ath, Richard
929.5   PN6291

ISBN 0–7137–1995–8

Typeset by Inforum Ltd, Portsmouth
Printed and bound in Great Britain by
Cox & Wyman Ltd, Reading

INTRODUCTION

by Spike Milligan

Since time began, man has held death in various states of emotional and intellectual dilemma and awe. What was it, an end or a beginning? The most positive thing he's done, is to disdain it; i.e. great acts of heroism in the face of danger. Even to this day, the greatest and most revered awards are ones for heroism – in America, the Congressional Medal of Honour, and our own, older, Victoria Cross. But in many philosophies (and my own) the answer is laughter, but this has only been a comparatively recent innovation in man's approach to death. Round about AD 1500 mildly humorous remarks started to appear on tombstones:

> Here lyes Margaret Young
> Who had sheed lived
> Would surely been hung
> By the length of her tongue.

Now this was a daring innovation when you consider the awe of say *Australopithecus* – who reverently bound the deceased in the sitting position, smeared the corpse with red clay, hoping that the colour and position of the body might deceive the Doppelganger into believing the corpse to be still alive – or the incredible finery of the dead Pharaohs. The thought of a comic comment on the pyramids would have been greeted with horror, even death.

But, as I say, since 1500 (ish) there has been a genuine progress in cutting back the 'Reaper's' grisly image by a change of emphasis, until, in 1800, you get genuine comic gems like this:

> Here lies the body
> Of Mabel Charlotte
> Born a virgin
> Died a harlot
> She was a virgin
> Till her 21st year
> A remarkable thing
> In Oxfordshire.

It shows a psychological courage as against the obvious physical one; for the hero who beat death, the danger was over – but not for the village joker who, on the following epitaph:

> Pray you all
> For the Vicar's daughter
> Millicent Ann
> Who died as pure
> As the day she began

then added,

> Not afore, in this village,
> She had every man.

He must have looked over his shoulder of a dark night for many a year!

I myself have never desecrated a tombstone, not even in fun, but I had cause to concoct an epitaph. During the war in North Africa I befriended a wild dog – we called him Havelock Ellis. No one was sadder than I when he was shot in the head one dark

night when he attacked a sentry, so I wrote:

> Here lies the body
> of Havelock the dog
> Shot thru the head
> And dropped like a log
> If he'd have been smart
> And not bit Gunner Fred
> This little dog
> Would not be dead.

I was heartbroken at his death – and yet it seemed better he had a funny epitaph when he died.

Man will forever be battling against death – sometimes with horrific results. I have seen old people who were no more than slow pulsating vegetables – *they* wanted to go, if they were told they were going to be put to sleep they would have been *happy*. There is a time to live, a time to die, a time to laugh, and at no time are the three of them very far apart.

I myself have my epitaph. It will read:

'I demand a Second Opinion.'

Read this book which has obviously been put together with love and gales of laughter, and buy a few for your friends, the older the better. Why not lie down in the garden with this book and a shovel, and make up your own epitaph? Better still, make up one about someone you hate, like the Inland Revenue:

> The man who ruined me for life
> Was this damn Tax Inspector
> But he tripped and fell upon a knife
> And now he's just a spectre.

And, remember, you'll never get to heaven alive!

8

I
TOMBSTONED

Here lies John Bunn,
Who was killed by a gun,
His name wasn't Bunn, but his real
    name was Wood,
But Wood wouldn't rhyme with gun, so
    I thought Bunn should.
> *From a gravestone in Southampton,*
> *Hampshire*

Sacred to the memory of
MAJOR JAMES BRUSH, Royal Artillery
who was killed by the accidental
discharge
of a pistol by his orderly, 14th April, 1831
Well done, good and faithful servant.
> *In Woolwich churchyard, London*

9

Erected to the memory of
JOHN PHILLIPS
Accidentally Shot
As a mark of affection by his brother.
On a gravestone in Ulster

Against his will
Here lies George Hill.
  Who from a cliff
  Fell down quite stiff.
When it happened is not known,
Therefore not mentioned on this tomb.
In St Peter's churchyard, Isle of Thanet

In memory of the Clerk's son:
Bless my i
Here I lies,
In a sad pickle
Killed by an icicle.
From a grave in Brampton Parish
Church, Devon

10

Here lie the bones of Lazy Fred,
Who wasted precious time in bed.
Some plaster fell down on his head,
And thanks be praised – our Freddie's
    dead.

*On the tomb of Frederick Twitchell in
Leeds, Yorkshire*

Here lies Tommy Montague
Whose love for angling daily grew;
He died regretted, while late out,
    To make a capture of a trout.
In Sutton Mallet cemetery, Somerset

Here lies poor but honest Bryan Tunstall,
    He was a most expert angler,
Until Death, envious of his mark,
    Threw out his line, hooked him and
        landed him here.
From Whitby cemetery, Yorkshire

Here lies John Dalyrymple
He picked a pimple.
On a grave in Thrustonville, America

11

Here lies a man who was killed by
    lighting;
He died when his prospects seemed to be
    brightening.
He might have cut a flash in this world of
    trouble,
But the flash cut him, and he lies in the
    stubble.
In Great Torrington churchyard, Devon

One Thomas buried here whose fate
    was such,
To lose his life by wrestling much
Which may a warning be to all
If they into such Pastimes fall.
On Thomas Hawkins, who died at 28, in
Mary Tavy, Devon

Here lies the body of Andrew Gear,
Whose mouth did stretch from ear to ear;
Stranger, step lightly o'er his head,
For if he gapes, by Josh, you're dead!
From a tomb in a Sunderland cemetery

12

Constance Bevon, wife of John,
Lies beneath this marble stone;
Fat and buxom, round and stout,
'Twas apoplexy bowled her out.
From a disappeared grave in Cumbria

Blown Upward
Out of Sight
He Sought The Leak
By Candlelight
On a headstone in Collingbourne Ducis,
Wiltshire

In Memory of
ELLEN SHANNON
Who was fatally burned by
the explosion of a lamp filled with
Danforth's Non-Explosive Fluid.
In Girard cemetery, Pennsylvania,
America

13

Here lies old
Aunt HANNAH PROCTER
Who purged but didn't call the Doctor.
   She couldn't stay
   She had to go
Praise be to God from whom
   All blessings flow.

In Queenborough cemetery, Medway,
Kent

She was not smart; she was not fair,
But hearts with grief are swellin'
All empty stands her little chair,
She died of eatin' watermelon.

From Teaneck cemetery, America

In Memory of
THOMAS FROST
Who died of Cholera Morbus
caused by eating green fruit
In the certain hope of a
blessed immortality
Reader, go thou and do likewise.

In Grantham churchyard, Lincolnshire

14

He Got a Fishbone in his Throat
Which made him sing an Angel's note.
On a headstone in Beacon Falls, America

Here I lies with my two daughters,
    Killed by drinking Cheltenham Waters;
If we had stuck to Epsom Salts,
    We wouldn't be lying in these vaults.
                On a headstone in St Giles' Church,
                Cheltenham, Gloucestershire

Here lie the bones of Joseph Jones,
    Who ate while he was able;
But, once o'erfed, he dropped down dead,
    And fell beneath the table.
When from the tomb, to meet his doom,
    He rises amidst sinners;
Since he must dwell, in Heaven or Hell,
    Take him – which gives best dinners!
                On a headstone in Wolverhampton
                Church, Staffordshire

15

Under this stone
Lies a Reverend Drone;
Who preached against sin
With a terrible grin;
In which some may think that he acted
 but oddly,
Since he lived by the wicked and not by
 the godly.

From Newgate, London

Here lies cut down like unripe fruit
 The wife of DEACON AMOS SHUTE
She died of drinking too much coffee
 Anny Dominy 1840.

On a grave in Bedrule Parish Church,
Roxburgh

Grim Death took me without any
 warning,
I was well at night
And dead at nine in the morning!

On a tomb in Sevenoaks churchyard,
Kent

16

Here lies the body of Mary Ann Lowder,
She burst while drinking a Seidlitz
    Powder:
Called from this world to her Heavenly
    rest:
She drank it and she effervesced.
            In Burlington cemetery, America

He called Bill Smith
A Lier.
            On a wooden headboard in
            Cripple Creek, America

Here lies the body of P.M. Haskell,
He lived a knave and died a rascal.
            From a disappeared grave in Islington,
            London

OWEN MOORE
Gone away
Ow'n more
Than he could pay.
            In St John's Church, Battersea, London

Mary had a little waist,
　　She laced it smaller still;
A stone o'er Mary has been placed
Out on the silent hill.
And on that stone these words are writ,
　　'Oh, let us hope she's gone,
Where angels never care a bit,
　　'Bout what they have got on!'
　　Epitaph on the dangers of lacing a corset
　　too tight. In the West Riding of Yorshire

Beneath this stone a lump of clay,
Lies Uncle PETER DANIELS.
Too early in the month of May,
He took off his Winter flannels.
　　　　　　　　In Chatham cemetery, Kent

Here lies poor Charlotte,
Who died no Harlot;
But in her Virginity,
At the age of Nineteen,
In this vicinity
Is rarely to be found or seen.
　　　　　　　On a headstone in Cardiff cemetery

Here lies
HERMINA KUNTZ
To Virtue Quite Unknown.
Jesus Rejoice!
At Last She Sleeps Alone.
At Belle Isle, America

In this here grave ye see before ye
   Lies buried up a dismal story
A young maiden crossed in love
And taken to the realms above.
But he that crossed her, I should say,
Deserves to go the other way!
In Pentewan graveyard, Cornwall

Little Willy in the best of sashes,
Played with fire and was burnt to ashes!
Very soon the room got chilly,
But no one liked to poke poor Willy!
From a cemetery in Montana, America

Oped my eyes, took a peep;
Didn't like it, went to sleep.
On an infant's grave in Worcester

19

Here lie the
Jones Boys Twins
As Dead as Nits:
One died of Fever
One of Fits.
On a grave in Sierra City cemetery,
America

Beneath this stone our baby lies,
He neither cries nor hollers;
He lived on earth just twenty days,
And cost us forty dollars.
From Burlington, America

God works wonders now and then;
  Here lies a lawyer and an honest man.

To which an unknown hand has added:

  This is a mere law quibble, not a
          wonder;
Here lies a lawyer, and his client under.
From a memorial stone in Walworth, London

20

Here I lie at the Chapel door,
Here lie I because I'm poor,
The farther in the more you'll pay,
Here lie I as warm as they.

On the tomb of Robert Phillip
(commonly called 'Bone' on account
of being the chief parish
grave-digger) at the Priest's Door,
Kingsbridge Church, Devon

Here lies JOHN HIGLEY
Whose father and mother were drowned
on their passage from America.
Had both lived, they would be
buried here.

In Belturbet churchyard, Ireland

Stranger, pause and shed a tear,
For May Jane lies buried here,
Mingled in a most surprising manner,
With Susan, Joy and portions of Hannah!

On a memorial plaque noting the
reburial of the ashes of four wives
spilled from their urns during a storm.
In Ringwood churchyard, Kent

GRAVE THOUGHTS

Remember me as you pass by
As you are now, so once was I,
As I am now, you soon will be,
Therefore prepare to follow me.

To which was later added:

To follow you I'm not content
Until I know which way you went.
   On a grave in Great Burstead Church, Essex

Life is a jest, and all things show it;
I thought so once, now I know it.
        On tomb of the poet John Gay in
                Westminster Abbey

Here I lie and no wonder I'm dead,
For the wheel of the waggon went over
   my head.
        On a grave in Prendergast churchyard,
                Dyfed

22

He lived and died a true Christian,
He loved his friends, and hated his
enemies.

In Dundee, Tayside

'All flesh is grass'
The Scriptures they do say,
    All grass when dead
      Is turned into hay.
Now when the reapers her away do take
My, what a whopping haystack she will
make!

*From the headstone of an exceedingly
fat woman in Kersey, Suffolk*

The horse bit the parson,
    How came that to pass?
The horse heard the parson say,
    All flesh is grass!

*On Reverend Michael Jones' tomb at
Welwyn, Hertfordshire*

23

Here lies one who for medicines would
    not give
    A little gold, and so his life he lost;
I fancy now he'd wish again to live,
    Could he but guess how much his
    funeral cost.

In Sheffield cemetery, Yorkshire

Whoever here on Sunday,
    Will practise playing at ball,
It may be before Monday,
    The Devil will have you all!

On a stone in the graveyard in
Llanvair Discoed, Gwent

An honest fellow here is laid,
His debts in full he always paid;
And, what's more strange, the neighbours
    tell us,
He always brought back borrowed
    umbrellas.

From a tomb in Los Angeles, California,
America

24

Underneath his ancient mill
Lies the body of poor Will;
Odd he lived and odd he died,
And at his funeral nobody cried;
Where he's gone and how he fares,
Nobody knows, and nobody cares.

In Canterbury cemetery, Kent

We must all die, there is no doubt;
Your glass is running – mine is out.

On a monument in Shoreditch
churchyard, London

If there is a future world
    My lot will not be bliss;
But if there is no other
    I've made the most of this.

From Desingwoke cemetery, America

25

Here lies the body of
   JAMES ROBINSON
and RUTH, his wife.
'Lord, their warfare is accomplished.'
On a grave in St Saviour's Church,
Hackney, London

Here lies my poor wife,
   A sad slatern and shrew,
If I said I regretted her
   I should lie too.
On a headstone in Texas, America

Reader, pass on, nor waste your
   precious time
On bad biography and murdered rhyme:
What I was before's well known to my
   neighbours
What I am now is no concern of yours.
On the grave of William Ash at
West Down, Devon

Here lies my poor wife, without bed or
    blanket
But dead as a door nail. God by thankit.
                    In Bradford cemetery, Yorkshire

Here is my much loved Celia laid,
At rest from all her earthly labours!
Glory to God! Peace to the Dead!
And to the ears of all her neighbours.
                    On a tomb in Southampton graveyard

Beneath this stone lies Katherine,
    my wife,
In death my comfort, and my plague
    through life.
Oh, liberty! But soft, I must not boast,
She'll haunt me else, by jingo, with
    her ghost!
                    On the tomb of Katherine Leary in Belfast

Here lies the mother of children seven,
  Three on earth and four in Heaven;
The four in Heaven preferring rather
  To die with mother than live with
    father.
At Godolphin Cross Church, Cornwall

  ELIZA ANN
  Has gone to rest.
She now reclines on Abraham's breast:
Peace at last for Eliza Ann,
But not for Father Abraham.
In Farmington cemetery, America

Beneath this stone and not above it
Lie the remains of Anna Lovett;
Be pleased, dear reader, not to shove it,
Lest she should come again above it.
For 'twixt you and I, no one does covet
To see again this Anna Lovett.
On a grave in Enfield, Greater London

28

Here lies my wife in earthly mould,
Who when she lived did nought but scold.
Peace! wake her not for now she's still;
She had, but now I have my will.
In Ellon churchyard, Grampian

Here lies Mary, the wife of John Ford,
We hope her soul is gone to the Lord;
But if for Hell she has chang'd this life
She had better be there than be
John Ford's wife.
At Potterne cemetery, Wiltshire

This stone was raised to Sarah Ford
Not Sarah's virtues to record
For they're well known by all the town
No, Lord, it was raised to keep her
down.
In Kilmory cemetery, Scotland

To free me from domestic strife
Death called at my house,
But he spake with my wife.
On a grave in Hadleigh, Suffolk

The children of Israel wanted bread,
  And the Lord he sent them manna,
Old Clerk Wallace wanted a wife,
  And the Devil he sent him Anna

On the grave of John Wallace,
Parish Clerk, of Ribbesford, Bewdley,
Hereford

He died in peace
His wife died first.
On a grave in Ilfracombe cemetery,
Devon

Beneath this stone and lumps of clay
  lies ISBELLA YOUNG
Who, on the 24th of May,
Began to hold her tongue.

From a disappeared grave in the
West Midlands

Here snug in grave my wife doth lie!
Now she's at rest, and so am I.

In Old Greyfriars, Edinburgh

When dear papa went up to Heaven,
  What grief mama endured;
And yet that grief was softened, for
  Papa was insured.

From a grave in Montreal, Canada

I plant these shrubs upon your grave,
  dear wife,
That something on this spot may boast
  of life.
Shrubs must wither and all earth must rot;
Shrubs may revive, but you, thank
  Heaven, will not.

On a grave in Rhayader, Powys

Charity, wife of Gideon Bligh,
Underneath this stone doth lie,
Naught was she ever known to do
That her husband told her to.

At St Michael Penkevil Church, Devon

31

We lived one and twenty years,
    Like man and wife together;
I could no longer have her here,
    She's gone – I know not whither.
If I could guess, I do profess
    (I speak it not to flatter),
Of all the women in the world,
    I never could come at her!
Her body is bestowed well,
    A handsome grave doth hide her.
And sure her soul is not in hell –
    The Fiend could ne'er abide her!
I think she mounted up on high,
    For in the last great thunder,
Methought I heard a voice on high,
    Rending the clouds in sunder.

On the tomb of a lady named Phillips
in Putney, London

Here lies Margaret Sexton,
Who never did aught to vex one.
Not like the woman under the next
    stone.

On the grave of a second wife at
Enfield cemetery, Greater London

32

Underneath this turf doth lie,
Back to back, my wife and I.
Generous stranger, spare the tear,
For could she speak, I cannot hear.
Happier far than when in life,
Free from noise, and free from strife.
When the last trump the air shall fill,
If she gets up, I'll even lie still.

At Halstead Church, Essex

Grieve not for me, my husband dear,
I am not dead, but sleeping here;
With patience wait, prepare to die,
And in a short time you'll come to I.

To which the husband has replied:

I am not grieved, my dearest life;
Sleep on, I have got another wife,
Therefore I cannot come to thee,
For I must go and live with she.

In Hertford cemetery

33

Stranger, call this not
    A Place of Doom,
To me it is a Pleasant Spot,
    My Husband's Tomb.

> *From a disappeared grave in*
> *Worcestershire*

When Miss Smith was twenty
She had lovers in plenty;
When Miss Smith got older
Her lovers got colder;
Then came Serjeant Spankie
And Miss Smith said thankie.

> *On the grave of Catherine Smith who*
> *beguiled a mean and ageing Scotsman*
> *out of his wealth. In Edinburgh*

To the Memory of
    JARED BATES
His widow, aged 24,
lives at 7, Elm Street,
Has every qualification for a Good Wife
    And yearns to be comforted.

> *At Aurora Falls, America*

Who far below this tomb doth rest,
Has joined the army of the blest.
The Lord has ta'en her to the sky:
The saints rejoice, and so do I.

In Cherening-le-Clay churchyard, Dorset

Here lies the body of Martha Dias,
Always noisy and not very pious.
Who lived to the age of three score and
   ten,
And gave to the worms what she refused
   to men.

From a disappeared grave in Shropshire

Here lies JANE SMITH
Wife of THOMAS SMITH, Marble Cutter.
   This monument erected
      by her husband
As a Tribute to her Memory.

Monuments of this style
   are $250.

From Annapolis cemetery, America

This spot's the sweetest
   I've seen in my life
For it raises my flowers
   And covers my wife.
In Llanelly cemetery, Gwent

Here lies
JOHN GIBBONS
'Peace, perfect Peace'

To which was added on the death of his wife:

'Till We Meet Again'.
In Northampton cemetery

She lived with her husband 50 years
And died in the confident hope of a
   better life.
On a grave in Easingwold Church,
Yorkshire

36

Jonathan Grober
died dead sober.
Lord, They Wonders Never Cease.
From a grave in San Francisco, America

Here lies
WILLIAM TEAGUE
Lover of his bottle
Murdered by the meanness of his wife
Chairman of the local Anti-Saloon League
and Dr Amos Throttle.
In Greeley graveyard, America

'Twas as she tript from cask to cask,
In at a bung-hole she quickly fell,
Suffocation was her task,
She had no time to say farewell.
On the grave of barmaid Ann Collins
at King's Stanley, Gloucestershire

Here lies John Steere,
Who, when living, brewed good beer,
Turn to the right, go down the hill,
His son keeps up the business still.
In Dagenham cemetery, Essex

Here sleeps in peace a Hampshire
  grenadier,
Who caught his death by drinking cold,
  small beer.
Soldiers! Take heed from his untimely fall,
And when you're hot, drink strong, or
  none at all!

To which was later added:

An honest soldier never is forgot,
Whether he die by musket or by pot.
                    On the grave of Thomas Fletcher in
                                          Winchester

Enclosed within this narrow stall,
Lies one who was a friend to *awl*.
He saved bad **soles** from getting worse,
But damned his own without remorse,
And though a drunken life he passed,
Yet saved **his sole**, by **mending at the
  last.**
                    On the grave of John Peters, a drunken
                              cobbler of Manchester

38

Here lies the Landlord of 'The Lion',
He hopes removed to the lands of Sion,
His wife, resigned to Heaven's will,
Will carry on the business still.

To which was added two years later:

Here lies the Landlord's loving wife,
Her soul removed from lands of strife.
She's gone aloft her spouse to tell
The Inn he left her turned out well.
                    In Bideford churchyard, Devon

Here lyes – read it with your hats on
The Bones of Bailie William Watson,
Who was moderate in his thinking,
And famous for his drinking.
                    *On the monument to a Glasgow
                    magistrate*

Here lieth Sir Thomas Jay, Knight,
Who, being dead, I upon his grave did
    shite
                    Discovered on a grave at Poole, Dorset

39

Dead drunk old Susan oft was found;
But now she's laid beneath the ground,
    As door-nail dead – alas the day!
Her nose was red, and moist as clay.
    From morn to night, of care bereft,
She plied her glass, and wet her throttle,
    Without a sigh her friends she left
But much she griev'd to leave her bottle.

*On a disappeared grave of
Susan Webster in Somerset*

Here, Reader, you may plainly see,
That wit nor humour can be proof
    against mortality.

*On a grave at Mancroft Church, Norwich,
Norfolk*

Here lies the wife of Simon Stokes,
Who lived and died – like other folks.

In Stratford cemetery, London

Here lies the good old knight Sir Harry,
Who loved well, but would not marry.

*On the grave of an amorous man at
Ditchley churchyard, Oxford*

Here lies Sir John Plumpudding of the
    Grange.
Who hanged himself one morning for a
    change.

From a disappeared grave in
Northumberland

Here lies the corpse of Dr Chard
Who filled up half of this churchyard.

On the grave of Thomas Chard in Yeovil,
Somerset

Here lies my adviser, Dr Sim,
And those he healed – near him.

In Grimsby Parish Church, Humberside

Stephen and Time are now both even,
Stephen beats Time, but now Time's
    beating Stephen.

On the headstone of a musician at St Ives,
Cornwall

Stranger, tread this ground with gravity,
Dentist Brown is filling his last cavity.

On a tomb in St George's Church
Edinburgh

41

He lived and died,
By suicide.

*On the grave of a Coroner who hanged
himself at West Grinstead, London*

Visitors tread gently
Here lies Doctor Bentley.

*In Great Haywood churchyard,
Staffordshire*

God works a wonder now and then,
Here, though a lawyer, was an honest
  man.

In Pineton churchyard, Norfolk

Here lies Stephen Rumbold, who lived
  to 101, Sanguine & Strong,
An hundred to one you don't live so long!

*In Brightwell Baldwin churchyard,
Oxfordshire*

42

Here lies John Trott, by trade a bum;
When he died the devil cry'd – Come,
    John, come.

On the grave of John Trott, a bailiff
of Hackney, London

DAVID WINTER

Here lies Mr Winter, collector of taxes,
I'd advise you to pay him whatever he
    axes;
Excuses won't do, he stands no sort of
    flummery,
Tho' Winter his name is, his process is
    summary.

In Eastcheap graveyard, London

BILL THOMSON

Here Lies Pecos Bill
    He always lied
    And he always will.
    He once lied loud
    And now lies still.

On a tombstone in Grand Forks, America

43

ELLEN GEE

Peerless yet hapless maid of Q,
   Accomplished L N G,
Never again shall I and U
   Together sip our T.

For, ah! the fates I know not Y,
   Sent midst the flowers a B,
Which ven'mous stung her in the I,
   So that she could not C.

Ye nymphs of Q, then shun each B,
   List to the reason Y,
For should a B C U at T,
   He'll surely sting your I.

Now in a grave L deep in Q,
   She's cold as cold can B,
Whilst robins sing upon A U,
   Her dirge and L E G

On the grave of a woman who died of a
bee sting in Kew, Surrey

44

Here lie the remains of John Hall,
   Grocer,
The world is not worth a **fig** and I have
   good **raisins** for saying so!
                    In Dunmore churchyard, Ireland

Hurrah! my boys, at the Parson's fall,
For if he'd lived, he'd a-buried us all!
            In Taibach churchyard, W. Glamorgan

Poems and epitaphs are but stuff,
Here lies Bob Barras and that's enough.
         On a headstone in Croydon cemetery, Surrey

He is not here, but only his pod;
He shelled out his peas and went to
   his God.
                    *On the grave of Zekiel Peace in
                             Nantucket, America*

   Here lies John Ross,
      Kicked by a Hoss.
On a grave in Kendal Parish Church, Cumbria

Some have children, some have none;
Here lies the mother of 21.
On the headstone of Ann Jennings, in
Wolstanston cemetery, Cheshire

ANN MANN
Here lies Ann Mann
She lived an old maid
And died an old Mann.
In Barton Moss cemetery, nr.
Manchester

DOCTOR IVAN LETSOME
When people's ill they come to I,
  I physics, bleeds, and sweats 'em;
Sometimes they live, sometimes they die;
  What's that to I? Letsome.
In San Francisco, America

PHILIP BOX
Here lies one Box within another,
The one of wood was very good,
We cannot say so much for t'other.
On a headstone in Leeds cemetery,
Yorkshire

JEMMY WYATT

At rest beneath this churchyard stone,
Lies stingy Jemmy Wyatt;
He died one morning just at ten,
And saved a dinner by it!

On a disappeared grave in Studley
churchyard, Wiltshire

LETTUCE MANNING

Oh, Cruel Death,
To satisfy thy palate,
Cut down our Lettuce,
To make a salad.

In Moulton churchyard, Cambridgeshire

PETER ROBINSON

Here lies the preacher, judge
    And poet, Peter:
Who broke the laws of
    God and Man
    And meter.

On a headstone in Bristol cemetery, Avon

47

JONATHAN THOMPSON
A good Husband and affectionate Father
Whose disconsolate Widow and Orphans
Continue to carry on the Tripe and
   Trotter business
  At the same shop as before their
  bereavement
From Shoreditch graveyard, London

And finally:

THOMAS DE'ATH
Death levels all, both high and low,
  Without regard to stations;
    Yet why complain
    If **we** are slain?
For here lies one at least to show
  He kills his own relations!
*From the grave of a relative of the
author in Huddersfield, Yorkshire*

2

WHERE THERE'S A WILL THERE'S A RELATIVE

The earliest existing will containing a touch of humour was written about AD156 by the eccentric, impoverished philosopher, Eudamidas of Corinth. It was actually preserved by the Greek writer, Lucian, who, of course, was responsible for producing a new form of literature – humorous dialogue. Apparently, on account of his poverty, Eudamidas had very little he could bequeath to his two closest friends, Arethaeus and Charixenes, and indeed what he *did* give them many people might think of dubious worth:

'I bequeath to Arethaeus my mother to support; and I pray him to have a tender care of her declining years.

'I bequeath to Charixenes my daughter to marry, and to give her to that end the best portion he can afford.

'Should either happen to die, I beg the other to undertake both charges.'

*   *   *

An Italian priest with a renowned sense of fun called 'Arlotto, the Parson', left instructions in his will dated 1483 that the following words were to be inscribed on his tomb:

'This supulchre was made by the parson Arlotto for himself – and for any other man who may desire to enter therein.'

*   *   *

The French satirist, François Rabelais (1494–1553) wrote with typical humour in the will he made in 1550:

'I have no available property, I owe a great deal, and the rest I give to the poor.'

The aptly named Alice Love of Rye in Sussex lived up to her name when she came to make her will in 1506, bequeathing several items of jewellery and clothing to her young lovers, including one very special bequest:

'And to Thomas Oxenbridge, my best girdle, which bound me but never denied him.'

* * *

Apart from being the greatest of our playwrights, William Shakespeare was also a man of wit, as this extract from his will made in Stratford-upon-Avon in 1616 reveals:

'*Item.* I give unto my wife my second bed, with the furniture.'

(It was Shakespeare's daughters, Susanna and Judith, who received his best bed – along with most of the rest of his furniture, property and wealth.)

51

The humorous Italian writer, Alessandro Tassoni, could not resist a joke or two in his will of 1612, declaring that he was 'sound in body and mind, save and except that singular fever which torments all human beings and makes them wish to survive their deaths'. He continued:

'My wish would be that my funeral should only employ one priest, that there should be simply the small cross and a single candle, and that as regards expense no more shall be incurred than will pay for a sack to stuff my remains into, and a porter to carry it.

'I bequeath to the parish in which I may be buried twelve gold crowns, without the smallest condition; the gift appearing to me very triffling, and, moreover, that I only give it because I cannot carry it away.

'And to my natural son named Marzio, whose mother is a certain Lucia of Garfagnano, I leave a hundred crowns in carlinos, that he may dissipate them at the wine-shop.'

Philip, the Earl of Pembroke and a
supporter of King Charles, took a violent
dislike to the author of a book about Oliver
Cromwell, and remembered the man in these
amusing words from his will of 1657:

'*Item*. I bequeath to Thomas May, whose
nose I did break at a masquerade, five
shillings. My intention had been to give him
more; but all who shall have seen his
History of the Parliament will consider that
even this sum is too large.'

* * *

Valentine Goodman, a resident of Hallton,
Leicestershire, was a man who lived up to his
name, though his choice of words to describe
those who were to benefit from his bequest
made in 1684 were certainly not the most
tactful:

'I bequeath the sum of £800 to be laid out
in land and the profits therefrom given each

year to the most indigent, poorest, aged, decrepid, miserable paupers of the district. And I decree that if any part of the money is employed for easing town levels, or not according to the intent of my bequest, then the gift must cease and the money employed for the redemption of Turkish captives.'

     ★   ★   ★

The wild and promiscuous life of his French wife, Charlotte, caused Henry, the Earl of Stafford, who was exiled with James II at the end of the seventeenth century, to declare in his will:

'To the worst of women, Claude Charlotte de Grammont, unfortunately my wife, guilty as she is of all crimes, I leave five-and-forty brass halfpence, which will buy a pullet for her supper. A better gift than her father can make her; for I have

54

known when, having not the money, neither had he the credit for such a purchase; he being the worst of men, and his wife the worst of women, in all debaucheries. Had I known their characters I would never have married their daughter, and made myself unhappy.'

＊　　＊　　＊

A devout old churchgoer, John Rudge of Trysull, Staffordshire, who had evidently witnessed the offences which he left a bequest to prevent, wrote in his will of 17 April, 1725:

'*Item*. I do also bequeath the sum of twenty shillings a-year, payable at five shillings a quarter, to a poor man to go about the parish church of Trysull, during sermon, to keep people awake, and to keep dogs out of the church.'

＊　　＊　　＊

Hated towards a neighbour was clearly expressed by John Swain of Southwark, London, who made this bequest in his will of 1765:

'*Item*. **To my neighbour, John Abbot, and Mary his wife, six pence each, to buy for them a noose, for fear the sheriffs should not be provided.'**

*   *   *

Dennis Tolam, a somewhat comical Irishman who lived in Cork, was believed to have hoarded away a fortune during his lifetime, which naturally aroused great interest among his relatives when his will was read in 1769. Their initial excitement, however, began to dwindle as the old man's 'bequests' were declared:

'*Item*. **I leave to my sister-in-law four old stockings which will be found under my matress, to the right.**

'*Item*. To my nephew, Michael Tarles, two odd socks and a green nightcap.

'*Item*. To Lieutenant John Stein, a blue stocking with my red cloak.

'*Item*. To my cousin, Barbara Dolan, an old boot with a red flannel pocket.

'*Item*. To Hannah, my housekeeper, my broken water-jug.'

(As the disappointed heirs were about to leave the room, the housekeeper Hannah indignantly dropped the old water jug. It cracked open to reveal a hoard of coins. And when the others carefully examined their 'bequests', each in turn found large sums of money concealed inside. The comic had had his last laugh!)

* * *

A man interested in the furtherance of marriage as well as horse racing made this peculiar bequest in his will dated 30 May, 1772. John Perram of Newmarket, England declared that his estate was to be realised so that:

57

'A marriage portion of £20 may be given
to a parishioner of this parish who on
Thursday in the Easter week, be married at
the church to a woman belonging to it;
neither party to be under twenty, nor to
exceed twenty-five years of age, nor be
worth £20; the trustees to attend in the
vestry to receive claims and pay the bequest
to such couples as should be qualified to
receive it.

'In the case of no claimants, then the
money, for that year only, to be paid by the
trustees to the winner of the next town
horse-race; the race course at Newmarket
is four miles long and is regarded the finest
in the world.'

*   *   *

Quite the reverse attitude was taken by an
English nobleman, Lord Chesterfield, who
had a godson evidently addicted to gambling
on the horses, for he inserted this punishing
clause in his will of 1773:

58

'In case my said godson, Philip Stanhome, shall, at any time hereafter keep, or be concerned in keeping of, any racehorse, or pack of hounds, or reside one night at Newmarket, that infamous seminary of iniquity and ill-manners, during the course of races there; or shall resort to the said races, or shall lose, in any one day, at any game or bet whatsoever, the sum of £500; then, in any of the cases aforesaid, it is my express will that he, my said godson, shall forfeit and pay out of my estate the sum of £5,000 for the use of the Dean and Chapter of Westminster.'

* * *

So incensed was the unknown recipient of the 'bequest' in the following will made by John Hylett Stow in 1781 that he took out a suit for libel and successfully obtained considerable damages for defamation from the dead man's estate: a factor which undoubtedly gave *him* the last laugh on his malicious benefactor.

'I hereby direct my executors to lay out five guineas in the purchase of a picture of the viper biting the benevolent hand of the person who saved him from perishing in the snow, if the same can be bought for the money; and that they do, in memory of me, present it to ———, Esq., a king's counsel, whereby he may have frequent opportunities of contemplating it, and, by a comparison between that and his own virtue, be able to form a certain judgement which is best and most profitable, a grateful remembrance of past friendship and almost parental regard, or ingratitude and insolence. This I direct to be presented to him in lieu of a legacy of three thousand pounds I had by a former will, now revoked and burned, left him.'

* * *

By a strange twist of fate an Englishman named Thomas Williamson who nursed a deep-seated hatred of the Irish was bequeathed a large piece of property in

60

Tipperary – but only on the condition he lived on the land. Grudgingly accepting the condition, Williamson nevertheless managed to cause equal surprise among his relatives when his own will was opened on 17 March, 1791 to disclose the following instructions:

'I give and bequeath the annual sum of ten pounds, to be paid in perpetuity out of my estate, to the following purpose. It is my will and pleasure that this sum shall be spent in the purchase of a certain quantity of the liquor vulgarly called whisky, and it shall be publicly given out that a certain number of persons, Irish only, not to exceed twenty, who may choose to assemble in the cemetery in which I shall be interred, on the anniversary of my death, shall have the same distributed to them. Further, it is my desire that each shall receive it by half-a-pint at a time till the whole is consumed, each being likewise provided with a stout oaken stick and a knife, and that they shall drink it all on the

spot. **Knowing what I know of the Irish character, my conviction is, that with these materials given, they will not fail to destroy each other, and when in the course of time the race comes to be exterminated, this neighbourhood at least may, perhaps, be colonised by civilised and respectable Englishmen.'**

* * *

The Countess of Loudoun also made his gruesome and rather mysterious request in her will in 1798:

'After my death I direct my right hand to be cut off, and buried in Donnington Park, at the bend of the hill toward the Trent, with this motto over it: "I byde my tyme".'

* * *

A member of the landed gentry, John Withipol of Walthamstow, near London, left

all his property and estate to his wife, declaring in his will of 1798:

'Trusting – yea, I may say, as I think, assuring myself – that she will marry no man, for fear to meet with so evil a husband as I have been to her.'

* * *

Before going to sea in 1804, Scottish seaman Duncan Forbes drew up his will in Aberdeen and requested his executor:

'In the event of my decease, to pay my wife one shilling, that she might buy hazelnuts, as she has always preferred cracking nuts to mending my clothes.'

* * *

In the curious will of John Tuke of Wath, near Rotherham, England, who died in 1810, the old man bequeathed:

'1 shilling to every poor woman in Wath; 10s 6d, to the ringers to ring a peal of grandbobs, which are to strike off while I am being put in my grave; forty dozen penny loaves to be thrown down from the church leads on Christmas Day forever. Also £1 1s per annum to the old woman who has for eleven years tucked me up in bed; and one penny to every child that attends my funeral.'

(According to local tradition, between 600 and 700 children turned up to claim their penny!)

* * *

From the will of a London merchant, James Porter, who left legacies to all his servants *except* his steward. He declared of this man in 1811:

'Having been in my service in that capacity twenty years, I have too high an opinion of his shrewdness to suppose he has not already sufficiently enriched *himself*.'

64

An eccentric London doctor, Thomas Ellerby, left explicit instructions about the disposal of his corpse – and a dire threat if his wishes were not carried out, as his will of February 1827 reveals:

'*Item*. I desire that immediately after my death my body shall be carried to the Anatomical Museum in Aldersgate Street, and shall be there dissected by Drs Lawrence, Tyrell, and Wardrop.

'*Item*. I bequeath my heart to Mr W., anatomist; my lungs to Mr R., and my brains to Mr F., in order that they may preserve them from decomposition.

'And I declare that if these gentlemen shall fail faithfully to execute these my last wishes in this respect I will come – if it should be by any means possible – and torment them until they shall comply.'

*   *   *

What seemed at first sight like a generous bequest to a wife had a sting in its tail in this will made in May 1833 by John Caldecott of Walworth, London:

'I leave my widow the sum of five hundred pounds. But she is only to come into the enjoyment of it after her death – in order that she may be buried suitably as my widow.'

* * *

A Hungarian opera lover, Stanislas Polzmarz, decided to try to encourage a rather bashful young friend named Lotz, whom he believed could be a fine opera singer, to perform publicly, and to this end inserted the following curious clause in his will made in 1835:

'I hereby bequeath the sum of three million florins to the aforementioned Lotz on the condition that before claiming it he

shall engage himself at the Scala Theatre in Milan to perform in the operas of *Othello* and *La Sonnambula*. Having heard him, at an evening party, sing fragments of the parts of Elvino and Othello, and admired the beauty of his tenor, I believe he can become a favourite of the whole musical world.

'If, therefore, I am right, he will thank me, and so will all *dilettanti*, for my acumen; if, on the other hand, he should fail, he will have money enough to compensate for the hisses he may incur.'

*   *   *

One of the very first wills published after Queen Victoria came to the throne was that of a typically strict parent leaving a considerable inheritance to his only daughter – but with the severest penalty if she did not follow his curious rules about female modesty. The Reverend Ebenezer Potts, the rector of

Whitby in Yorkshire, addressed himself thus
to his daughter, Anna, in his will of 1837:

'Seeing that my daughter Anna has not
availed herself of my advice touching the
objectionable practice of going about with
her arms bare up to the elbows, my will is
that, should she continue after my death in
this violation of the modesty of her sex, all
the goods, chattels, moneys, land and other
property that I have devised to her for the
maintenance of her future life shall pass to
the oldest of the sons of my sister, Caroline.
Should anyone take exception to this my
wish as being too severe, I answer that
license in dress in a woman is a mark of a
depraved mind.'

* * *

Despite his enormous wealth, Richard
Watson, of Surrey, felt miserly towards at
least one of his servants, instructing his
executors in his will of 1838:

'To ensure that the night shirt in which I am laid out be not a new one but an old one – as it will become the perquisite of the nurse.'

* * *

The will of the eccentric and extremely wealthy French nobleman, the Marquis D'Aligre, made in 1847, contained a number of amusing bequests, including one of 20,000 francs to a faithful retainer to take care of his four pet rats! Among the others were:

'I leave 200,000 francs a year to the "Phalansterians", but they are only to receive this sum on the day in which they shall have transformed the ocean into orangeade, and gratified mankind with that appendage he needs to make him equal to the gibbon.

'To Mme N . . . , who was full of attention for me, I leave one broken cup. And I declare that all the while she thought

she was taking me in, I was laughing in my
sleeve at the grimace she would make when
she discovered it was I who had got all her
little gifts – her smiles and favours – and
had no intention of repaying them as she
expected.

'I withdraw from M.A. . . . and M.V . . .,
the sums I had left them by a former will;
they have so often proclaimed that I am a
man who would cut a farthing in four, that I
would on no account oblige them to change
their opinion.

'Finally, I leave to my relatives, oblivion;
to my friends, ingratitude; to God, my soul.
As for my body, it belongs to my family
vault.'

       *   *   *

William Kinsett of London expressed the
desire in his will of October 1855, that his
body should be burned after his death. As
this request predates the now commonplace

70

practice of cremation, his instructions make interesting, not to say ultimately amusing, reading:

'Believing in the impolicy of interring the dead amidst the living, and as an example to others, I give my body, four days after death, to the directors of the Imperial Gas Company, London, to be placed in one of their retorts and consumed to ashes, and that they be paid ten pounds by my executors for the trouble this act will impose upon them for so doing. Should a defence of fanaticism and superstition prevent their granting this my request, then my executors must submit to have my remains buried, in the plainest manner possible, in my family grave in St John's Wood Cemetery, *to assist in poisoning the living in that neighbourhood.*

*   *   *

A wealthy London landowner with an abhorence of moustaches gave a solemn warning as to the consequences of his sons wearing them in his will of 1862:

'In case my son Edward shall wear moustaches, then the devise hereinbefore contained in favour of him, his appointees, heirs, and assigns of my said estate called Pepper Park, Twickenham, shall be void; and I devise the same estate to my son William, his appointees, heirs and assigns. And in case my said son William shall wear moustaches, then the devise hereinbefore contained in favour of him, his appointees, heirs and assigns of my said estate called Pepper Park, Twickenham, shall be void; and I devise the said estate to my said son, Edward, his appointees, heirs, and assigns.'

* * *

A passionate temperance fighter and fitness fanatic, James Sargeant of Leicester, in

England, bequeathed his estate to his two idle and dissipated nephews, but only on the following stringent conditions laid down in his will of 1871:

'As my nephews are fond of indulging themselves in bed in the morning, and as I wish them to prove to the satisfaction of my executors that they have got out of bed in the morning, and either employed themselves in business or taken exercise in the open air, from five to eight o'clock every morning from the fifth of April to the 10th of October, being three hours every day, and from seven to nine o'clock in the morning from the 10th of October to the 5th of April, being two hours every morning; this is to be done for some years, during the first seven years to the satisfaction of my executors, who may excuse them in case of illness, but the task must be made up when they are well, and if they will not do this, they shall not receive any share of my property. Temperance makes the faculties clear, and

exercise makes them vigorous. It is temperance and exercise that can alone ensure the fittest state for mental or bodily exertion.'

*   *   *

A man of high ideals but limited resources to carry them out was an eccentric Bristol clergyman, the Reverend William Hill, who died in November 1875, leaving his estate of £3,000 towards the destruction of the British Empire and the prevention of drinking. He wrote in his will:

'I pray for the king of Zion to overthrow the politico-ecclesiastical establishment of the British Empire, and I leave the world with a full conviction that such prayer must ere long be answered.

'I likewise declare that the drinking customs of professors and non-professors are doomed, and trust that Heaven will dash this work of the Devil from earth.'

A husband who found the words to express his displeasure towards his wife but could not deprive her of at least a small portion of his estate was a London bookseller, Edward Parker, who wrote in 1785:

'I bequeath the sum of £50 to Elizabeth whom, through my foolish fondness, I made my wife, without regard to family, fame or fortune; and who, in return, has not spared, most unjustly, to accuse me of every crime regarding human nature, save highway robbery.'

*   *   *

A Parisian eccentric, Monsieur Benôit, of the Rue des Gravillers, filed these instructions with the notary of the French capital in his will of October 1877:

'I expressly and formally desire that my remains may be enclosed for burial in my large leather trunk, instead of putting my

survivors to the expense of a coffin. I am
attached to that trunk, which has gone
round the world with me three times.'

*   *   *

Old watches have been popular legacies for
generations, but there can have been few
stranger bequests than that of Peter
MacAndrews of Glasgow to his son in
January 1877:

**'I bequeath my two worst watches to my
son, because I know he is sure to dissect
them.'**

*   *   *

Being worth their weight in gold was made
literally true in the case of two Scottish girls
whose father – turning upside down the idea
that all his race are mean – made this
provision in his will in 1877. Thomas Black of
Kilmarnock declared:

'And as for my daughters, M . . . and J . . . , I direct that my executor should have them weighed, and then give to each the equivalent weight in one pound bank notes.'

(The younger girl, who was somewhat plump, did better than her older sister, receiving £57,344 from the will, while the other got a mere £51,200!)

*　　*　　*

A Yorkshire mill-owner named Thomas Keighley who had a large family and a great many relatives decided on this novel way of dividing his estate, according to his will made in 1879:

'I therefore declare that my executor is empowered to divide my properties among only those of my descendants who are permanently resident in the said county of Yorkshire and also measure not less than six feet four inches in height.'

An elderly Canadian, Doctor Dunlop, of Winnipeg, Canada, made some stinging remarks on the characters of his various beneficiaries in his will published in 1879:

'To my eldest sister Joan, my five-acre field, to console her for being married to a man she is obliged to henpeck.

'To my second sister Sally, the cottage that stands beyond the said field with its garden, because as no one is likely to marry her it will be large enough to lodge her.

'To my third sister Kate, the family Bible, recommending her to learn as much of its spirit as she already knows of its letter, that she may become a better Christian.

'To my fourth sister Mary, my grandmother's silver snuff-box, that she may not be ashamed to take snuff before company.

'To my fifth sister, Lydia, my silver drinking-cup for reasons known to herself.

'To my brother Ben, my books, that he

may learn to read with them.

'To my brother James, my big silver watch, that he can know the hour at which men ought to rise from their beds.

'To my brother-in-law Jack, a punch-bowl, because he will do credit to it.

'To my brother-in-law Christopher, my best pipe, out of gratitude that he married my sister Maggie whom no man of taste would have taken.

'To my friend John Caddell, a silver teapot, that, being afflicted with a slatternly wife, he may therefrom drink tea to his comfort.

'To George Caddell, my friend's son, a silver tankard, which I would fain leave to old John himself lest he should commit the sacrilege of melting it down to make temperance medals.'

* * *

A man who prided himself on his sense of humour, Walter Allen of Kent, made a will in

1884 full of the most appalling puns, of which these instructions for the mode of his burial can be taken as typical:

'**The coffin is to be of red fir. I** *pine* **for nothing better. Even this may be thought a** *deal* **too good, though certainly not very** *spruce* **. . .'**

An American theatre attendant, John Reed, who silently nursed an ambition to appear on the stage of the Walnut Tree Theatre in Philadelphia where he worked for forty-years, achieved his life-long desire by this peculiar request in his will of 1887:

'**My head to be separated from my body immediately after my death; the latter to be buried in a grave; the former, duly macerated and prepared, to be brought to the theatre, where I have served all my life,**

and to be employed to represent the skull of Yorick – and to this end I bequeath my head to the properties.'

*　　*　　*

Broken-hearted lovers have written many bizarre last testaments before attempting, successfully or unsuccessfully, to commit suicide. Perhaps the strangest of all such wills was made by an unknown London man in 1894 and published a few years later by Dr Forbes Winslow of the Royal College of Surgeons who swore that it had been 'literally carried out':

'Having been crossed in love and determined to end an unhappy life, I desire that my body shall be boiled down and all the fat extracted therefrom. This fat is to be used in making a candle which is then to be presented to D . . . , the object of my affections, together with a letter enclosed

containing my farewells and expressions of undying love.

'I further desire that the candle and letter should be delivered at night, in order that my beloved might read these lines by the light of my dying love.'

* * *

William Vanderbilt, a relative of the famous American financier and railroad magnate, Cornelius Vanderbilt, gave one of the strangest reasons for a personal bequest in his will filed in 1896:

'I supplicate Miss B . . . to accept my whole fortune, too feeble an acknowledgement of the inexpressible sensation which the contemplation of her adorable nose has produced on me.'

* * *

82

William Farren, a Cambridge man with an evident grudge against the students of the town's famous university, made this declaration in his will published in 1900:

'I fervently hope that by the disposition of my property that my family are saved from keeping or living in an undergraduate lodging-house, as undergraduates are more like wolves and dogs than human beings.'

★ ★ ★

Virgil Harris, an American lawyer and collector of old wills, came across the last testament of an old Victorian bachelor made in 1901, in which the man asked for his property to be divided equally between three ladies.

'I declare that my wealth such as it is found to be, should be shared between the three ladies undermentioned, to whom I proposed marriage and each of whom

refused me. The reason for my bequest,
should any of these ladies enquire it, is that
by their refusal I owe them all my earthly
happiness.'

*   *   *

Despite the fact that the making of a will is
considered a serious business, quite a number
of people have chosen to make their last
testaments in verse – the earliest of these
being William Hunnis, an apparently sober
gentleman who served for much of his life as
the Chapel Master to Queen Elizabeth I. For
the first time in his life he felt the urge to
resort to poetry to express his final wishes:
and in so doing began a tradition which has
remained acceptable in the eyes of the law to
this day. Hunnis' will made about 1580
declared:

**To God my soule I do bequeathe, because
it is his own,**

My body to be layd in grave, where to my
   friends best knowen;
Executors I will none make, thereby great
   stryfe may grow,
Because the goods that I shall leave wyll
   not pay all I owe.

*   *   *

   A San Francisco millionairess who was
widely believed to prefer animals to human
beings confirmed this notion when her will
was published in 1959. Mrs Amy Bachman
wrote:

   'I leave the sum of $600,000 to
establish a memorial fund for my deceased
terrier "Bingo".
   'To the San Francisco Society for the
Prevention of Cruelty to Animals, who shall
administer the memorial, and the other
animal charities hereunder listed, I
bequeath $336,000.
   'To my husband, Roger, I leave $1, and
my son, nothing.'

The largest single bequest to animals was made by Eleanor Ritchey, heiress to the Quaker State Refining Corporation, when she died in Fort Lauderdale, Florida, in 1968:

'I bequeath my entire estate, value estimated at $4.5 million, to my 150 stray dogs.'

(Perhaps, understandably, this will was contested by the woman's relatives, and by the time it was settled in September 1973, the estate had grown in value to $14 million, while the number of strays still living had shrunk to 73!)

* * *

An American dog-lover tried to protect the well-being of his pet with a special inducement in his will. Writing in 1973, Will Jonson of Maryland said:

'I hereby bequeath every damned thing I own that she wants to my wife, with the

following stipulation: that my dog "Lobo" who is essentially the same temperament as I, be allowed more freedom than I have been allowed.'

* * *

Right at the start of the century, in 1801 in fact, an American physician, Dr Frederick Wagner of Connecticut, who had apparently been totally ignored by his family for much of the time while he was alive, gave vent to his macabre sense of humour in his final testament:

'To my relatives who, now that I am dying, cannot do too much for my comfort, I declare as follows. That to my brother, Napoleon Bonaparte, I bequeath my left arm and hand; to another brother, George Washington, my right arm and hand; and to my brother Lord Nelson my legs, nose and ears. And to this end I leave one thousand dollars for the dismembering of my body.'

This amusing clause appeared in the will of another doctor, Ian MacIntyre of Glasgow, published in 1902:

'To my wife, as a recompense for deserting me and leaving me in peace, I ask that my sister, Elizabeth, make her a gift of ten shillings sterling from my bequest, so that she is enabled to buy a pocket handkerchief to weep after my decease.'

*   *   *

A crochety old soldier, General Hawley, who also had something of a sense of humour, drew up his own will in London in 1907 because, he said, 'of the hatred and suspicion with which I regard all lawyers'. The document was accepted for probate, and in it the General left:

'The sum of £100 to my servant Elizabeth Buskett because she has proved herself a useful and agreeable handmaid.

88

'The remainder of my property I
bequeath to my adopted son, Arthur,
provided that he is not foolish enough to
marry the said Elizabeth – in which case
neither is to inherit a farthing.

'I further desire my executors to consign
my carcase to any place they please, and if
the parish priest should claim a burial fee,
they may let the puppy have it.'

*   *   *

A superstitious rural farmer in Finland,
Mat Jurgen Weins, who had apparently led
an evil and dissipated life, took what he
obviously considered to be the only course of
action when he came to dispose of his
property in his will, dated 1909:

'Having no family or relatives that I know
of, and being desirous of making the best
possible impression on him whose company
I expect to share in the next world, I hearby

89

bequeath my property, such as it is, to his
Satanic Majesty, the Devil.

'Should any claimant on my estate
present himself after I am gone, and my
executor have any doubts as to my
intentions, I rest assured that my inheritor
will know well enough how to dissuade such
a claimant.'

*(Strangely, though an heir to Weins' farm was
found, the man was so terrified by the threat
contained in the will that he refused to lodge any
claim against its provisions!)*

* * *

Mary Piper, a wealthy widow of Kansas
City, Missouri, ingeniously revenged herself
on her nephew, Rollins Bingham, who had at
first been a favourite and then displeased her.
In her will of 1910, she declared:

'I do leave to my nephew Rollins
Bingham, the sum of $2,500 to be held in

trust by my executor *until the death of my nephew and then applied to give him a proper burial.'*

* * *

An habitual drinker, E.J. Halley, of Memphis, Tennessee, divided what was left of a fortune he had inherited from an eccentric aunt among various acquaintances including a number of baseball players (his favourite sport), several bar tenders (who had supplied him with drinks), and three deputy sheriffs (who had seen him safely home when he was drunk). He also remembered several drinking companions, and, with notable generosity, two other people who helped him at what must have been critical moments – as his will of October 1910 vividly reveals:

'To the nurse who kindly removed a pink monkey from the foot of my bed – $5,000.

'To the cook at the hospital who removed snakes from my broth – $5,000.'

A French restaurant owner, Pierre Giffard, developed an abiding dislike for his fellow-countrymen, and made this very evident in his will filed in Marseilles in 1911:

'I declare that the French are a nation of dastards and fools, and I therefore bequeath the whole of my fortune to the people of London. I also desire that my body should be taken from this country and deposited into the sea a mile from the English coast.'

*   *   *

Martin Willow, a Londoner, found an ingenious way round a strange legacy bequeathed to him by an uncle in 1917. The will declared:

'To my nephew I leave the sum of £2,000, but on condition that half of this sum is to be placed beside me in my coffin and buried with me.'

Having assured himself from the executor that he would receive the money as long as the condition was carried out, the astute young man wrote out a cheque for £1,000 and gave it to the lawyer to place alongside his uncle's body. On it he wrote, 'Pay to Bearer'.

*   *   *

A London merchant banker, William Hampton, of Kew, anxious to impress upon his young son the need for careful study of financial matters, wrote in his will of 1918:

'I leave to my son a copy of Lawrie's *Interest Tables*, not for its intrinsic value, but in the hope that so small an incident may be of use to him in future years. And I particularly recommend to him the study of the compound interest tables, as showing that from comparatively small investments, by patience, large sums may be realised.'

*   *   *

93

Benjamin Werner, a millionaire Austrian, who had a life-long fear of darkness, made the following extraordinary provision in his will published in Vienna in 1921:

'Insomuch as I have a profound horror of darkness, I desire that my executors see that the vault in which I am placed is continually lighted by electricity, and that my coffin is similarly illumined, to which end I leave all the proceeds of my estate herebefore listed.'

*   *   *

An eccentric Bordeaux lawyer named Claude Benoit who many people had expected to leave his large fortune for the building of a school or municipal building in his memory, lived up to his reputation for doing the unexpected when his will was filed in 1926:

'I hereby direct and command that my executors convey the whole of my property, estimated at 100,000 francs, to the construction of a lunatic asylum, for I believe this to be an act of restitution to the clients who were insane enough to employ my services.'

* * *

A father, obviously unhappy at his daughter's choice of a husband, made what he must have felt was a fitting bequest in his will of 1927. James Harrow of Kensington declared:

'To my daughter I leave the sum of one hundred sovereigns which she is to spend on herself.
'To my son-in-law I leave my old walking stick in the hope that someone will give him a good thrashing.'

* * *

Daniel Ross of Michigan was remembered as the archetypal hen-pecked husband. He managed to have the last word, however, when he made his will in 1928:

'For my tyrannical wife, who did not give me any peace during the last twenty-four years since I was married to her, I leave **ONE DOLLAR** for which to buy a rope and hang herself. There was not a married man yet more miserable.'

*   *   *

The owner of a women's dress shop in Brighton, England, Andrew Evans, avenged himself on a nephew who had persistently teased him about his occupation, with this clause in his will published in 1948:

'And to C . . . H . . . , I bequeath the sum of £200, but before receiving it he must, in the presence of my executor, walk down the most important street in our fashionable resort dressed in female attire.'

Continuing the honourable tradition of having the last word on those nearest and supposedly dearest, American banker Evan Abrahamson, said in his will of 1964:

'To my wife I leave her lover and the knowledge that I wasn't the fool she thought I was.

'To my son I leave the pleasure of earning a living. For twenty-five years he thought the pleasure was mine, but he was mistaken.

'To my valet I leave the clothes he has been stealing from me regularly for ten years.

'And to my chauffer I leave my cars. He has almost ruined them, and I want him to have the satisfaction of finishing the job.'

* * *

Patriotism was demonstrated in the most positive terms by Miss Marjorie Jesson of Bournemouth, Dorset who, after a number of

bequests to her family, completed her will in
1971 with the words:

'**And the remaining sum of £20,000 I
bequeath to the Chancellor to assist in the
repayment of the national debt.**'

*   *   *

Philip Grundy, a Lancashire dentist,
demonstrated the same unbending attitudes
as his famous forebear, Mrs Grundy, when
his will was published in March 1974. For to
inherit the major part of his fortune of over
£180,000 his unmarried nurse had to observe
the following conditions:

'**That she must never use any lipstick or
any other make-up of any kind whatsoever
apart from clear nail varnish, and wear no
jewellery such as rings, earrings, necklaces,
and never go out with any men on her own,
or with a party of men, during a period of
five years. I want her to be happy, as she**

has been a real friend to me – and genuinely had my interest at heart.'

*   *   *

Edward Horley, a bachelor of Altrincham, who had spent a long and hard life working as a coal merchant, bitterly resented the money he had had to pay the tax man. He expressed this anger in his will of 1975, instructing his solicitor:

'Take what is left from my estate after the duty is paid and buy a lemon. This is to be cut in two: one half sent to the Income Tax Inspectorate and the other to my Tax Collector. With each, add the message, "Now squeeze this!" '

*   *   *

Two motorists obviously very strongly attached to their favourite cars gave instructions in their wills recently to have the

vehicles *buried with them!* In August 1975
when Mrs Margaret Griffiths of Ladybrand
in South Africa died, she left these directions:

**'To bury with me my 1948 Studebaker
Champion so that it might also rest.'**

*(There was, however, strong opposition to this
request on two counts. The car was said by
collectors to be a rare item – one of only nine left
in the country. While the undertaker protested he
could not bury the blue vehicle because 'the
cemetery is for whites only'.)*

* * *

The second devoted driver was the young
widow of a Texas oil millionaire, Mrs Sandra
West, of San Antonio, who in March 1977
left her entire $2.8 million estate to her
brother-in-law, Sol West, as long as he
complied with the following conditions:

'To dress my body in a lace nightgown and place it in my favourite car, a blue 1964 Ferrari, with the seat slanted comfortably.

'Should the said Sol West fail to carry out this request, he is to inherit only $10,000.'

(Although, again, this was disputed by relatives, a Los Angeles court ruled that the instructions should be carried out and Mrs West was duly buried in the Ferrari which was placed in a steel container and encased in concrete.)

* * *

A retired teacher, Ernest Digweed, of Portsmouth, made one of the most celebrated wills of recent years in 1976. After a lifetime spent living quietly in a small terrace house, and with no known relatives, he left his estate of £25,107 in trust:

'To be paid to the Lord Jesus Christ in the event of a Second Coming. My estate is to be invested for 80 years, and if during

101

those 80 years the Lord Jesus Christ shall
come to reign on Earth, then the Public
Trustee, upon obtaining proof which shall
satisfy them of his identity, shall pay to the
Lord Jesus Christ all the property which
they hold on his behalf.'

*(A further clause in the will stated that the
accumulated interest on the estate was to go to the
Crown after twenty-one years, and if Christ had
not appeared within eighty years the Crown was
to inherit everything.)*

*   *   *

An American sea fisherman, Don Mobelin,
of New York, thought he might continue to
be of use to his fellow anglers after his death,
and gave special instructions to his executor
in his will of 1983:

'I request that my ashes be thrown onto
the shoals of New York bay where I have
often fished with my friends of the Bronx

Fishing Club in the hope that they might attract the fish and enable me to give my friends one more good catch.'

*   *   *

A similar outrageous sense of humour was revealed in the will of Tory Gribble of Bristol who asked in his will of June 1983:

'That my ashes may be used in the family's egg timer so that I shall continue to be of use after my death.'

*   *   *

And, finally, my own favourite humorous will – which I might well have written myself if Tom Goodison of Norwich in Norfolk had not thought of it first in April 1983 – who asked for all his relatives and friends attending his funeral to be given an envelope containing a one pound note on which were written the instructions:

'Have a smoke and crack a joke. Thanks for coming.'

3
DIED LAUGHING

'There's worse to come' has proved literally and often grimly true, and there are few better examples with which to begin a section of the more outlandish cases of this kind, than the story of Major Walter Summerford.

In 1918, while fighting in Flanders, Major Summerford was struck by lightning, thrown from his horse, and as a result of his injuries was invalided out of the Army.

Six years later, back in his native Canada, he was hit again by lightning while fishing near Vancouver. And in 1930 all the odds about lightning never striking twice, let alone three times, were overturned when *another* bolt struck him and left him paralysed!

Major Summerford died in 1932 and was laid to rest in a secluded grave not far from

Vancouver. Then, two years later, nature played her final trick – a shaft of lightning struck the poor Major's grave and completely shattered his headstone!

*   *   *

During an outbreak of fighting at an isolated outpost on the Mons front also during the First World War, a German soldier named Heinz Müller shot and killed an English soldier in the opposing trenches.

Later, as Müller advanced with some other German troops to the English lines, he found the body of the man he had killed still upright, his rifle aimed to fire and his now cold finger still poised on the trigger.

Deciding to take the dead man's rifle as a souvenir of his success, Müller wrestled with the stiff fingers to release the weapon. As he did so, the rifle suddenly went off and shot him dead through the heart!

*   *   *

As David Anthony was driving home to Liverpool in March 1936, he suddenly came around a sharp bend and found to his horror another car racing towards him on the wrong side of the road.

Desperately, David slammed on his brakes, but his car skidded uncontrollably and the two vehicles collided head on.

When David regained consciousness in hospital, he was thankful to learn he had escaped the terrible accident with only minor cuts and bruises. The other motorist, too, had also miraculously survived.

But there had been a passenger in the other car and he was dead. And the unfortunate man turned out to be David Anthony's twin brother, Paul . . .

* * *

Some weeks after Igor Ravenko had undergone a stomach operation in Moscow in 1949, he returned to hospital complaining of more abdominal pains. For a second time he

was operated on, and the medical team discovered the previous surgeon had inadvertently left a pair of clamps in Igor's stomach.

Happy at this discovery, Igor returned to his family. A month later the poor fellow was dead.

At the autopsy he was opened up once more. And this time in his stomach was discovered a surgical gauze pad which the second surgeon had left behind!

*　　*　　*

Luigi Ercolli chose the most horrendous way of committing suicide in 1959 – he decided to set fire to himself on a deserted headland not far from his home in Nardo, southern Italy.

No sooner had he begun his grisly ritual, however, than Luigi had second thoughts. Frantically, he began to roll about on the ground and beat at the flames.

In his terror, though, he forgot where he

was – and suddenly fell over the edge of the headland and plunged to his death on the rocks below . . .

★   ★   ★

The most bizarre case of a near fatal motoring accident occurred in the Ténéré desert in the Niger, in 1960.

A French soldier, Henri Le Queux, was driving an army lorry across this vast, sandy wilderness when he rammed a tree and overturned the vehicle. Reports said he was lucky to escape with his life.

The tree was the only one within a radius of fifteen miles!

★   ★   ★

While suffering from acute depression, Walter Alexander, a Chicago engineer, drove to a local motel in March 1966 intent on committing suicide. In one of the bedrooms

he took out a revolver and shot himself three times in the head.

Some hours later Walter awoke to find he was still alive and feeling rather better. He decided to return home and tell his wife the injuries to his head had been caused by a fall. Miraculously, all three bullets had passed straight through his head.

A week later, however, Walter received a visit from the police. They had found the three bullets from his revolver in the wall of the motel bedroom.

On admitting to his incredible escape from death, he was promptly charged with causing criminal damage.

*   *   *

California Carol Hargis set out with dedicated and ingenious efficiency to kill her unfortunate husband, Harry, in 1968.

First, she gave him a massive dose of LSD. This did no more than give him a mind-bending trip.

Next, she dosed a blackberry pie with the venom of a tarantula – but still he survived.

Equally unsuccessful was sabotaging his car with a home-made bomb (it failed to go off) and attaching a live electric wire to his shower.

Once again she returned to poor Harry's food – dosing his beer with tranquilisers, but he thought the drink was off and threw it away. When he fell ill from all these unpleasant attentions, Carol even tried injecting air into his veins.

She finally succeeded in her objective – and earned a life sentence – by the simple expedient of striking him on the head with an iron bar.

★　　★　　★

Tired of all the violence in the streets of her native Belfast, Mrs Elizabeth McClelland emigrated around the world to New Zealand in 1970.

Tragically, just two years later, in

February 1972, Mrs McClelland was rushed
into a Christchurch hospital suffering from
head injuries from which she subsequently
died.

Police inquiries established that her
injuries had been caused by being struck on
the head by a placard carried by a
demonstrator who was protesting on behalf of
Irish Civil Rights.

*   *   *

After his wife had left him, John Stratton of
Manchester saw no point in going on living.
He decided to commit suicide in 1973, and
having carefully sealed the doors and
windows of his home, turned on the gas oven.

Although the fumes soon engulfed the
house, because the supply was North Sea gas,
it proved non-toxic. This lucky escape made
Stratton have second thoughts.

Perhaps he would give life another chance.
He took a cigar from the mantelpiece and lit
it.

111

At this, the highly inflammable North Sea gas exploded him and his house into smithereens.

* * *

As Woodrow Creekmore was driving to his home in Chickasha, Oklahoma, in 1976, his car suddenly slewed across the road and hit a telegraph pole. Amazingly, he was able to get out of the virtually demolished vehicle without a scratch.

However, as he stood discussing the accident with a police patrolman who appeared on the scene, the telegraph pole suddenly toppled over and, striking Woodrow on the head, killed him instantly.

* * *

In February 1976, a Belgian doctor, Herman le Compte, claimed that he had devised a rejuvenation treatment which would enable people to live for 1,000 years.

The police were not impressed by his statement that he was able to arrest the natural deterioration of the body's organs by massive injections and exercise – and arrested him. He was placed in jail in Bruges to await trial for practising medicine while debarred.

Then while he waited, 'Dr Long Life' – as he was nicknamed – suffered a heart attack . . .

* * *

When Billy Vecchio of Chicago stole a car to impress his girlfriend in August 1976, he ended up with a very different ride from the one he had expected.

During his little outing, the car broke down and Vecchio hailed a passer-by to give him a push. The man, Joe White, just happened to be the real owner of the car!

Vecchio, however, laughed at the other man's claim and proceeded to punch White, a night-club bouncer by profession, on the nose.

Before he repossessed his vehicle – White

later explained to a local court – he broke
both Vecchio's wrists, fractured his jaw, and
then stabbed him. The joy-rider
subsequently died of his injuries.

*　　*　　*

According to the *Detroit Free Press*, in July
1977, Mr Michael Maryn of Passaic in New
Jersey had been mugged eighty-three times
during the previous five years.

He had been shot twice, stabbed, coshed,
lost part of one ear, had his nose broken, his
ribs smashed and his skull fractured. In
addition to his injuries, he had lost numerous
bags of groceries, four cars and over $2,000 in
cash.

'I don't worry about it,' Mr Maryn told the
newspaper, 'I'm lucky in one respect – I have
a blood clot in my leg that keeps me from
travelling far from home.'

*　　*　　*

An Italian named Abel Ruiz felt the world

had ended when he was jilted in June 1978.

In his despair he hurled himself in front of the Genoa–Madrid Express. But, miraculously, he fell between the rails and sustained only minor injuries.

After being treated at the Genoa hospital, the self-destructive Abel tried suicide a second time. This time he leapt in front of a lorry. Again, he was only slightly injured by the impact.

Following further treatment at the hospital, he was only released on the understanding that he would not try to kill himself again.

But, within the hour, he was back once more. This time, though, the incident was a genuine accident: he had been struck by a runaway horse. And now his injuries *were* serious.

The following day the man who wanted to commit suicide was dead – accidentally!

* * *

Like many people, Herman Holt worried

about his income tax. Indeed, when the 55-year-old chip shop owner from Halifax, Australia, received a letter from the Revenue in 1980, he became convinced he had fallen foul of the authorities and decided to kill himself rather than face disgrace. The following day he was found dead by a railway line.

In actual fact the letter had nothing to do with arrears – it was the Revenue admitting they owed *him* A$1,400!

*   *   *

After months of trying to find a job, Romolo Ribolla, grew so dejected he decided to kill himself. On the morning of 4 April 1981, as he sat in the kitchen of his home near Pisa, he suddenly produced a gun from his pocket and told his wife he was going to shoot himself.

For nearly an hour, the distraught woman pleaded with Romolo until, overcome with emotion at her entreaties, he burst into tears and flung the revolver to the floor.

But as it struck the ground, the gun went off and shot Mrs Ribolla dead.

116

A man described as 'The Most Accident-Prone Person in Britain' made a habit of spending every Friday the thirteenth in bed for his own safety, according to a report published in November 1981.

For in the space of five years, Robert Renphrey, a Peterborough bus driver, had suffered one calamity after another on this fateful Friday. He had been: Involved in five car crashes and four bus breakdowns.
Fallen into a river and been knocked down by a motorcycle.
And even walked through a plate glass door!

*   *   *

Giuseppe Saraniti was convinced his wife was having an affair with Salvatore Manganaro. And in March 1983 he confronted the other man in his home in Genoa, Italy, brandishing a revolver.

Falling to his knees, Salvatore swore that the story was not true. He had never touched Maria Saraniti. But Giuseppe was not

convinced and thrust the revolver against the frightened man's temple.

Salvatore closed his eyes and clutched at the gold pendant of the Virgin Mary hanging around his neck. 'Mother of Jesus,' he pleaded, 'give him a sign I am telling the truth.'

Giuseppe pulled the trigger. But nothing happened, only a dull click.

Now it was Giuseppe's turn to be frightened and he ran to the police station in Genoa and confessed what he had tried to do. After he had been charged with attempted murder, a police spokesman said, 'The strange thing was there was nothing wrong with the gun. It was fully loaded and worked perfectly when we tested it!'

★   ★   ★

A man aptly named Hi Woe was rushed naked into a hospital in Peking in February 1983 with a metal spittoon stuck on his head.

According to the ambulancemen who

118

brought him in, the spittoon – a common item in Chinese bedrooms – had been playfully plonked on his head by his wife while the couple were making love.

Although the doctors battled hard to save the young man's life, he died of asphixiation before he could be freed. Later, it was learned the previous evening had been his wedding night!

*   *   *

Mike Stewart, the president of the Auto Convoy Company in Dallas, Texas, was so convinced of the dangers that a number of low-level bridges in the city presented to traffic, that in April 1983 he decided to make a movie about the problem to convince the authorities.

Hiring a camera crew, he proceeded to drive around Dallas on the back of one of his trucks to film the potential death spots. As he did so, the truck went underneath one of the bridges in question and he was decapitated.

An attractive 16-year-old Israeli girl was taken to court in Tel Aviv in September 1983 and ordered to stop walking around her home in the nude.

The complainant was not a neighbour, but the girl's 80-year-old stepfather. Her provocative displays were to give him a heart attack, he said, so that she could inherit his fortune!

*   *   *

A French couple appeared in court at Bobigny near Paris in September 1984 charged with trying to murder each other.

The 60-year-old husband had been awoken suddenly in the night by a severe electric shock. Leaning over the bed was his wife, who was wearing rubber gloves and had attached an extension lead from the mains to his head. Over his heart a wet sheet had been laid.

Leaping from the bed, the man rushed to the next room, seized a rifle, and returned to shoot his wife in the thigh.

In court, it was explained that the man's poor eyesight had saved the life of the wife. And the electric shock had failed to kill him because the couple lived in one of the few streets in the area where Electricité de France provided a lower-powered system with less than the normal 220 volts which *would* have proved fatal!

*   *   *

Fate has played some cruel – and deadly – tricks on mankind. Take the case of New Yorker Joseph O'Malley. He was exceedingly drunk one night in 1953 and decided to take a short cut home along a subway railway line.

When, inevitably, nature called, O'Malley decided to pee right where he stood. Unfortunately, when the stream of urine hit the third rail of the track, 600 volts shot up into his body and he dropped dead.

*   *   *

Because thieves were constantly stealing

apples from her orchard, Mrs Laura Baines of Penzance in Cornwall decided to employ a nightwatchman to keep an eye out for the pilferers.

Unfortunately, Mrs Baines did not trust her employee and one night in 1959 she crept out into the orchard to make sure he was not asleep on the job.

The man shot her dead.

* * *

An elderly Swedish pastor met an unlikely end while engaged on church duties in the winter of 1955.

Pastor Karlo Toivio was baptising some new members of his church at the time – standing in a pool of heated water for the ceremony. Things went fatally wrong when his assistant clergyman handed him a live microphone . . .

* * *

Devoted birdwatcher Henry Humphret of

New York was finding extreme difficulty in 1963 in getting near enough to some swans living on High Shield Lake to ring them. In desperation, he decided to try to approach them by night *in disguise*.

Obtaining the hollowed-out body of a swan, he placed it over his head and waded into the lake just after midnight. Unfortunately he could not swim and drowned in the darkness.

*　　*　　*

An eccentric Californian inventor, Reuben Tice, of Monterey, was obsessed with creating a machine for taking the wrinkles out of prunes.

In November 1967, having perfected a piece of equipment which he hoped would perform such a task, he set it in motion. A mighty explosion followed.

Tice was discovered dead under the shattered remains of his machine and a huge pile of prunes. They were all still wrinkled.

123

Horror struck the Brazilian town of Goiânia in December 1973 when a column of killer ants a mile long and half a mile wide marched into the community. It took sixty firemen with flame throwers over fifteen hours to drive the ants back into the jungle.

In their wake they left the scant remains of several people they had devoured – including the chief of police.

* * *

So distraught did Mrs Vera Czermak of Prague become over her husband's infidelities that she decided to commit suicide from the window of her third-floor flat. On the morning of 25 July 1975 she hurled herself out . . . and landed on Mr Czermak who was returning unexpectedly to the flat. She survived unhurt – he was killed.

* * *

A freak storm ended six years of drought in

the Spanish Sahara in August 1975, leaving behind it a number of giant pools of water.

Into one of these, Mohammed Aliud fell and died – drowned in the middle of the desert.

* * *

Felix Hanaud, a 77-year-old Frenchman who had always received excellent medical care during his lifetime, decided to donate his body to science by giving it to the Toulouse University Medical Faculty.

In February 1976, some years after he had drawn up his will, Felix went into the University building, told the caretaker he could wait no longer – and shot himself through the head.

* * *

There was nothing that General Miguel Arracha, the head of the Anti-Urban Guerrilla Section of the Argentine Army,

enjoyed more than a game of dominoes.
Indeed, it was his habit to play each week at
his home in Buenos Aires with a friend,
General Carlos Mendoza.

But this came to an abrupt end in June
1976 when General Arracha was blown to
pieces by a bomb that his friend General
Mendoza left behind after one of their games!

*   *   *

Thoughts of love and romance were on the
mind of honeymooner Philip Ryan as he
walked back to his holiday cottage on
Reunion Island in the Indian Ocean, in June
1977. He had taken a short stroll in the
moonlight while his bride of one day was
preparing for bed.

With a gleeful love call Philip vaulted over
what he believed to be the fence surrounding
the cottage – and disappeared into the crater
of the Ganga volcano.

*   *   *

Keen angler José Hermanez accidentally struck a bees nest with his line while fishing from the banks of the Rio Negro not far from Sao Paolo, in August 1977. The infuriated bees immediately attacked José.

To escape, he leapt into the river – and was promptly devoured by piranha fish.

*   *   *

After undergoing a successful operation to have a replacement heart in November 1977, Mr George Least, a dairyman of Salisbury, Rhodesia, fell in love with a nurse who helped him through his convalescence.

When the girl did not return his love, Mr Least shot himself.

*   *   *

Former actress Eleanor Barry, 70, could not resist hoarding every newspaper, press cutting, book and souvenir which in any way related to her career. Over the years, this

collecting mania grew to such an extent that the house she shared with her sister in New York became jammed from floor to ceiling.

On 20 December 1977, she was found dead in the house – a huge pile of the books and newspapers had fallen on her.

* * *

Charged with aiding a suicide, salesman Marvin Redland told a curious story to a court in Norfolk, California, in December 1977. He had been discussing reincarnation with the barmaid of a club in town.

The woman had first told him she had been a canary in her previous life. The next time she returned to earth, she told Redland, she would be a buffalo.

'I admit that I laughed in her face,' the witness said. 'Greatly to my surprise she then shouted, "You may laugh, but I will prove it." At this she reached under the bar, took out a gun, and shot herself dead.'

An Australian snooker fan who desperately wanted to have a shot named after him spent years trying to come up with a new variation. In January 1979, Robert Fairtree of Melbourne finally cracked the problem.

He announced the 'Fairtree' which was made by a man suspended over the table with his legs fastened to the ceiling and helium balloons attached to his wrists. Sadly, when Robert gave a demonstration he crashed on to the table and died.

* * *

A Sri-Lankan woman's attraction for a snake proved fatal in Trincomalee in 1980. She had raised a cobra in the belief that it was her dead son reincarnated.

On 1 July the snake bit her and she died.

* * *

Attempts to find the oldest man in Asia in 1982 finally brought to light a 118-year-old

Malaysian with the extraordinary name Lebai
Omar Bin Datuk Panglima Garang. Nor was
that all that was extraordinary about him: he
was also living in sin with a teenage girl.

To celebrate his record, the old man agreed
to marry the girl. However, on his return
from the wedding ceremony riding a tandem
which some well-wishers had given him, with
his wife on the front, Lebai Omar fell off and
died.

* * *

A fetish for washing women's hair was the
undoing of a 29-year-old Italian, Luigi
Longhi, when he was brought before a court
in Soenderborg, Denmark, in March 1983.

Luigi was said to have had a life-long
craving for female tresses, and was confined
indefinitely for strangling Heike Freiheit, a
21-year-old West German hitch-hiker, whom
he had tied up and then washed her hair four
times before killing her.

* * *

The most unlikely murder weapon was
exhibited in a trial held in Wellington, New
Zealand, in April 1984.

Before the court was 53-year-old Malcolm
Francis, charged with beating his wife to
death with – a frozen sausage. He denied the
murder.

★　　★　　★

Olympic marathon hopeful, Richard
Mbelwa, 22, of Dar es Salaam in Tanzania,
had put in many hours of arduous training.
As he was running through a golf course on
the morning of 10 May 1984, a policeman
suddenly ran into sight and shot him dead.

The officer said later he thought Mbelwa
was a fleeing thief.

★　　★　　★

Two Chicago lawyers arguing the respective
merits of certain athletes in forthcoming
Olympic Games in July 1984 decided to settle

their dispute by racing each other down a
hallway in their law firm.

One of the men, who had poor eyesight,
crashed through a 39th-floor window and fell
to his death.

* * *

A 34-year-old Yugoslav, Vebi Limani, died
near his home on Sara Mountain in August
1984 when he was struck by lightning.

Reporting his death, the local newspaper
Politika said he was the fourth member of his
family to die in the past six years. His father,
brother and uncle had all passed on –
similarly struck dead by lightning.

* * *

Barbecuing was one of the passions shared by
Diane Fellman and her husband, Jim, at their
palatial American home in San Jose.

But when they fell out of love in August
1984, Diane shot poor Jim. Afterward she
cooked his body on the barbecue and ate part
of his arm.

Fifty-seven-year-old Edward Hill was feeling pretty chipper as he left a Houston hospital in November 1984. He had just spent three weeks being treated for a minor heart complaint and was now declared fit.

As he crossed the foyer he was handed his bill for the treatment. He took one look – and dropped dead. The bill was for $38,000!

* * *

Over the years there have been some very apt and often humorous comments passed 'In Memoriam'. Here are some of the best of them.

The most bizarre final comment was surely that of a convicted English murderer, Edgar Edwards, as he was led to the scaffold in December 1902, condemned to death for killing John and Beatrice Darby.

As he mounted the steps, he said brightly to the hangman, 'I've been looking forward to this!'

* * *

133

Two American Army buddies were chopping wood together on fatigue duty at Fort Smith, Arkansas, in June 1922. Suddenly, Private Daniel McGranie remembered that his friend, Private Benjamin Clark, owed him ten dollars. He demanded the money back there and then.

Both men stopped chopping and an argument ensued. Clark denied ever having borrowed the money and refused McGranie's insistent demands.

All at once McGranie lifted his axe and with one blow severed his friend's head from his body.

'I just lost my head', was all he could mutter as he was taken in charge.

* * *

A deranged New Yorker, Ernest Walker, not only committed a totally motiveless crime in 1949, but also left an equally bizarre confession at the scene of the crime.

* * *

Walker lured a young messenger boy to his Manhattan apartment and clubbed him to death with an iron poker. He then left the body for the police to find with a note scrawled upon it:

'I expect you will be surprised to see what I have done.'

*　　*　　*

Police were somewhat baffled when they were called to the Ministry of Tourism Offices in Nairobi, Kenya, in June 1959, by a distraught clerk who said that a man was savagely attacking a *stuffed* lion.

The officers arrived to find the man pummelling the lion and shrieking abuse. He had apparently smashed the glass cage in which it was on display and then tried to strangle it.

Said one of the policemen later, 'When the man calmed down he told us his brother had been killed by a lion and he wanted revenge!'

Mischievous little 3-year-old George Semple
was being taken for a walk along the cliffs at
Brighton, in Sussex, by a family friend in
1960, when he tumbled over and was killed
on the rocks below.

Later, the friend confessed to the police
that she was responsible, having pushed
George over. 'He just would not behave,' she
said.

*   *   *

Few learner drivers showed more
determination than Mr David George of
Shanklin, in the Isle of Wight. Then
immediately upon being told he had passed
his test in July 1976, he collapsed over the
wheel of his car and died.

'It was his eighth attempt,' a sad instructor
said later.

*   *   *

In order to emphasise the terrible nature of
hanging, D.H. Beenan, a leading opponent of

capital punishment, was demonstrating just
what happened when it took place to an
audience in New Zealand, in 1976.

Slipping a noose which he had hanging
from a rafter around his neck, Mr Beenan
exclaimed, 'How horrible the whole thing is!'
– stepped from the chair he was standing
upon and accidentally hanged himself.

*   *   *

As he was taking photographs of the city
dump of Takapuna, also in New Zealand, for
a new brochure in July 1976, photographer
Peter Hammond became conscious of a
bulldozer coming in his direction. Anxious
not to interrupt the driver's work, Mr
Hammond stepped behind a pile of rubbish.

At this – said a policeman later giving
evidence into Mr Hammond's death – the
bulldozer driver brought his vehicle closer
and with incredible delicacy squashed the
photographer into the ground.

The driver later told the law, 'I hate
snoopers.'

In February 1977, a West German housewife,
Hilda Brunner of Frankfurt, was charged
with murdering her husband by putting rat
poison in his daily glass of beer for a period of
four years.

She confessed to the police, 'I only did it to
cure him of drinking.'

*   *   *

It was an open and shut case when Michael
Koukourakis appeared before a court in
Piraeus, Greece, in September 1977, charged
with murdering his wife's lover.

Michael was very ready to admit he shot
the man to death, but pleaded, 'I acted in an
instant of momentary sanity.'

The jury agreed and acquitted him.

*   *   *

When a group of Brazilian policemen raided a
party in Santiago after complaints that it had
been going on noisily for three days in May

1978, they found rather more than they expected. For sitting upright in one corner was a dead man.

Asked to explain, the host of the party said, 'He was a gate-crasher called Jose. We discovered that he was dead on Saturday evening. But not wanting to spoil the party we decided to leave him there until Monday morning.'

★   ★   ★

French farmer Pierre Trichard of Mexmieux was happily watching a game of World Cup football on television in June 1978 when his wife, Claudi, asked him to shell some peas for their supper.

Pierre refused, and despite several further entreaties, continued to stare resolutely at the TV set. At this, Claudi snatched her husband's shotgun from the wall, took aim, and blew his head off.

'I couldn't understand it,' Mme Trichard said later, 'France were already out of the competition.'

Football also shattered the happy home life of
a Yugoslavian couple in August 1982. While
Marinko Janevski, a retired policeman, was
watching a match on TV at his home in
Belgrade, his wife came into the room and
tried to stop him.

'I strangled her,' Marinko later admitted,
while standing trial for murder. 'I always get
excited when watching football.'

*   *   *

While Mrs Barbara Eastman was selling
flowers in Naysmith Square, Toronto, in
September 1978, she was suddenly
approached by a man who announced: 'I am
God – could you direct me to the nearest
church, please?'

Although somewhat taken aback, Mrs
Eastman gave the necessary instructions and
then watched in amazement at what
happened next – for as she later explained in
court:

'When I had given him the directions he

took off his hat, said "Thank you", stepped out into the road, and was instantly killed by a tractor.'

*　　*　　*

All his life, keen angler Jerry Head of Melbourne, Australia, had dreamed of catching a giant-size fish. When he did, it literally killed him – as his wife Rhoda told newpapermen in November 1978, after the family had marked his passing in a rather unusual way.

'He was out fishing with my son Doug when he landed a 58-pound cod.' said Mrs Head. 'The shock killed him. But after the funeral we had a fish supper – cod-fritters on a bed of clams with his name written in instant potato over the lot.'

*　　*　　*

After the unfortunate death of her father, Mrs Joan Spence gave evidence at a London inquest in March 1980.

'My father died after slipping on a bacon sandwich,' she told the court. 'As he was a life-long vegetarian I consider this to be a manifestation of divine injustice.'

* * *

The familiar situation of a husband falling out with his mother-in-law took on a new dimension in India, in April 1980.

For when Vekay Velayudhan appeared in a court in Poona charged with beheading his mother-in-law, he said simply in his defence: 'We had not been getting along for some time.'

* * *

Problems can also arise between parents and children – but hardly as bizarre as that which occurred in America, in October 1980. Before a New York juvenile court appeared 14-year-old Christine Martin who said that because her parents had complained when her pet

rabbit left droppings on their living-room carpet, she picked up her father's gun and shot them both to death.

'I have been having problems with them for some time,' she calmly added.

*　　*　　*

Mr Harry Olsen was understandably upset at the death of his wife, the former Miss Stella Walsh, an Olympic Gold and Bronze Medallist, who passed away at their home in southern California in December 1980.

But he was stunned by the revelation of the post-mortem that his 'wife' was, in fact, a man!

'We had been married for almost thirty years,' he said afterwards. 'I am 92, but I must have been a lot more innocent then than now.'

*　　*　　*

The 'shooting' of arch-villain J.R. Ewing in

143

the television soap opera 'Dallas' provoked as
many heated arguments as to who was
responsible both on-screen as well as off. In
Dallas itself, in March 1981, a couple named
Silverstone took their argument to the limit in
a grim reprise of the show itself.

So angry did the wife become at her
husband's refusal to agree with her verdict on
who was J.R.'s killer, that she walked out of
the living room, fetched a shotgun, and
slayed her husband.

'She was under some strain,' a relative told
police later.

* * *

A South African judge with the singularly
appropriate name of Justice W.J. Human was
addressing a man who had been found guilty
of rape, in August 1983.

Sentencing the prisoner, Rodney Axe, to
death, he added, 'I have treated you as
leniently as possible.'

* * *

144

At an inquest in Sheffield, Yorkshire, in
October 1983, into the death of a Mr Harry
Tanner, evidence was given by his brother
who had watched the whole incident.

John Tanner said that his brother had
climbed to the top of a 200-foot high bridge
and then with a wave of his hand and a shout
of 'Geronimo!' had plunged to his death in
the river Tees.

'He was a happy-go-lucky chap,' added Mr
Tanner.

*   *   *

Faces were red in Fort Lauderdale, Florida,
when a letter was sent out by the local social
security office in June 1984 to a woman of 61
who had died the previous December.

The letter, to a Mrs Pat Shamres, six
months after her death, contained a
handwritten addition which said, 'We have
received a report that you may be deceased.
Please come in with proof of identity.'

*   *   *

145

And now a few last words from the famous, beginning perhaps inevitably with Oscar Wilde (1854–1900) who, true to his reputation, is credited with not one but two exit lines on his death-bed. So you may take your choice from either.

'This wallpaper is killing me. One of us must go.'

Or else:

'Alas, I am dying beyond my means.'

* * *

The great South African statesman, Cecil Rhodes (1853–1902), took his final confinement will ill-concealed annoyance and his final words were to one of his secretaries:

'Turn me over, Jack.'

* * *

The enormously influential Russian playwright, Anton Chekhov (1860–1904), who died at the height of his powers had a suitably dry comment to make:

146

'It's a long time since I drank champagne.'
(Appropriately, the great man's coffin then
rode to burial in a freight car marked FRESH
OYSTERS!)

*   *   *

The brilliant American short story writer, O.
Henry (real name William Sydney Porter,
1962–1910), went out of this vale of tears
quoting from a popular song:

'Turn up the lights. I don't want to go
home in the dark.'

*   *   *

Efforts to make the great Russian writer and
mystic, Leo Tolstoy (1828–1910), seek
comfort from the Russian Orthodox Church
as he lay on his death-bed were met with this
sharp rejoinder – which was also his last:

'Even in the valley of the shadow of death,
two and two do not make six.'

*   *   *

Robert Erskine Childers (1870–1922), author of the classic spy thriller, *Riddle of the Sands* (1903) and a member of Sinn Fein, said, as he was about to be executed, with other patriots, by an Irish Free State firing squad:

'Take a step or two forwards, lads – it will be easier that way.'

* * *

The famous English novelist, Arnold Bennett (1867–1931), died in Paris of typhoid after drinking a glass of water. His last words were:

'The water is perfectly safe.'

* * *

Thomas Edison (1847–1931), the American inventor and man of vision, chose to look forward rather than back in his last words, informing those around his death-bed with tantalising emphasis:

'It's very beautiful over there.'

Oliver Wendell Holmes (1841–1935), the
great American judge, delighted in telling the
story of the last moments of one of his uncles,
John Holmes, who died in Boston. As the
man lay on his death-bed, a nurse who was
busy keeping his feet warm was heard to
remark, 'If his feet are warm, he is alive –
nobody ever died with his feet warm.'

At this, John Holmes suddenly sat up in
bed and said, 'John Rogers did!' Then he
died.

(John Rogers was an English Protestant
burned at the stake for heresy in 1555.)

*   *   *

The irrascible film comedian and life-long
agnostic W.C. Fields (1880–1946) was found
reading the Bible on his death-bed. Asked the
reason for this astonishing about-face, Fields
grumbled:

'I'm looking for a loop-hole!'

*   *   *

One of the funniest men of the twentieth century, humorist James Thurber (1894–1961), who shrugged off the blindness that inflicted his last years with comments like, 'I don't get distracted by the sight of a pretty girl – but of course I can still *hear* a pretty girl go by,' did not disappoint his admirers with his last words:

'God bless . . . God damn!'

* * *

The rumbustious Irish writer and notorious drinker, Brendan Behan (1923–64), passed his last remark to a nun comforting him on his death-bed:

'Ah, bless you Sister, may all your sons be Bishops.'

* * *

One of the finest British men of the law of this century, Lord Chief Justice Gordon Hewart (1870–1944), passed away on a fine spring morning with these words ringing around his room:

'Damn it! There's that cuckoo again!'

When the pioneer woman Member of Parliament and socialite, Nancy Astor (1879–1964), found herself surrounded by her children as she lay dying in her bed she demanded of them:

'Am I dying or is this my birthday?'

* * *

Tallulah Bankhead (1903–68), the American actress and a celebrated wit, was economic in her use of words and amusing in her demand when she died in New York City's St Luke's Hospital.

'Bourbon,' she said.

* * *

That master of wit and humour, Sir Noel Coward (1899–1976), did not disappoint his friends and admirers when it came to making his final *bon mot*:

'Goodnight, my darlings, I'll see you tomorrow,' he said.

'The King of Rock 'n' Roll', Elvis Presley (1935–77), despite the torment of his closing years remained a devout Christian to the end, and his last remark was singularly appropriate:

'We'll make this tour the best ever.'

*   *   *

American Pulitzer prize-winning author William Saroyan (1908–81) actually went to the trouble of telephoning the Associated Press with what were to be his last words:

'Everybody has got to die, but I have always believed an exception would be made in my case. Now what?'

*   *   *

The doctors at a New York Hospital were amazed when a 41-year-old patient, Donald Cohen, suddenly leapt out of his bed in March 1968. Their amazement was understandable: Donald had had two heart

attacks and the specialists had given him up for dead.

But that wasn't the only amazing thing about his recovery. He had a bizarre story to recount of his experiences 'on the other side'.

'I dreamt I was on a merry-go-round,' he said, 'and the angel of death was beckoning me. The carousel picked up speed, but I managed to resist the mysterious force that pulled me towards him.

'I jumped off – and found myself on the floor of the hospital ward!'

★　　　★　　　★

A Swedish doctor has devised the strangest set of scales imaginable according to a report published in 1969. Dr Nils Olof Jacobson believed it was possible to weigh the human soul and set about proving his theory by placing the hospital beds of dying patients on extremely sensitive scales.

From his research, said Dr Jacobson, he had established that at the precise moment of death the scales registered a decrease of just eight-tenths of an ounce!

Ugandan witch doctor, Dada M'Shuma, became famous throughout his country in the 1970s as 'The Man Who Can See The Future'. The old man was said to be able to make contact with the dead and also predict events that were to come.

Millions were said to believe implicitly in Dada, according to report – but sceptics claimed he got his knowledge of world affairs from a transistor radio hidden in his hut . . .

* * *

Anton Kjowski, a Polish immigrant who lived in Manchester, was obsessed with an ancient superstition that he had brought with him from the 'old country' he left over a quarter of a century earlier. He believed in vampires.

And because the traditional method of guarding against attack from vampires was to keep plenty of garlic about the house, Anton doubled his defences by sleeping with a clove of garlic in his mouth. Tragically, he was

wracked by coughing one night in April 1973,
dislodged the piece of garlic, and was choked
to death by the clove.

*   *   *

According to a 'Vampire Census' carried out
by the Vampire Research Centre in New
York in April 1983, there are thirty-five
people in the United States who consider
themselves to belong to the ranks of the
Living Undead.

Of these people, a third lived in the state of
California and one is an alien vampire –
having emigrated from Spain.

*   *   *

A ghost with a fascination for sexy movies
made his presence felt in a cinema in Bury,
Lancashire, in 1976. Nicknamed, 'Old Sid',
the spectre had a habit of appearing whenever
X-rated films were shown.

'Old Sid' had been seen around the cinema

for many years – but less in recent times until the advent of more explicit movies. Several times he was spotted dressed in medieval clothes and a three-cornered hat, hovering about six feet over the stalls.

Apparently what 'Old Sid' *didn't* like were horror movies . . .

* * *

Halfway through a séance on the top floor of the Spiritualists' Association headquarters in London, in March 1978, an insistent tapping was heard from outside a blacked-out window. Then a voice asked, 'Can I come in?'

The medium holding the séance promptly asked the spirit's name and a voice replied, 'Ken.'

For a moment there was a puzzled silence among those taking part in the séance, and then the voice spoke again: 'I've been repairing the roof and somebody's locked the window on me. Let me in!'

At this everyone present collapsed into

laughter, said secretary Tom Johanson later, and the 'ghost' was promptly let in from 'the other side'.

*   *   *

'Fred', the ghost who was reported to be haunting the Sapsford family of Larkfield, Kent, in August 1978, was a rather unusual kind of spirit – a high spirit, in fact. For according to the four people he suffered from B.O.

For fourteen years, the Sapsfords had been aware of 'Fred' who usually made his presence left by the unmistakable odour of sweaty feet. At other times he left behind the scent of sizzling bacon, burnt toast and roast coffee.

Said Mrs Joan Sapsford, 'We don't want him exorcised – just sanitised.'

4
GRAVE MOMENTS

An Irish undertaker on the scene of a railway accident in County Cork, in 1906, was reported to have told the two assistants who came with him to 'get the dead and the dying into coffins as quickly as possible'.

When one of the men pointed out that some of the victims were alive and might be saved, the man retorted sharply, 'Oh, bedad, if you were to pay any attention to what *they* say, not one of them would allow that he was dead!'

* * *

Retired doctor Omar Philips of Oklahoma was a fastidious man who had carefully arranged every aspect of his life right from his youth. He carried this attention to detail up

to the very moment of his death.

For prior to committing suicide with a shotgun in August 1938, he calmly telephoned a local funeral parlour and reported his imminent death – as well as giving instructions for his funeral!

* * *

The following report was carried by the *Daily Telegraph* in August 1960:

'Guests at Mr Henry Allen's barbecues in the garden of his house at Milford, New Jersey were upset by the sight of coffins being carried into the adjoining undertaker's premises.

'Mr Allen complained to the town council, which yesterday ordered the undertakers to erect a barrier of trees.'

* * *

It was the most embarrassing moment the

undertaker in Miami, Florida had ever
encountered.

A much respected local citizen had died in
May 1966, and a spacious tomb complete
with inscribed memorial stone had been
ordered and duly erected before the funeral.

It was just moments before the mourners
were due to arrive at the cemetery when a
horrified assistant pointed out to the firm the
terrible mistake that the stonemason had
made on the memorial stone.

For in the last name of A. Perfect Whitt the
W had become an S . . .

* * *

One of the most curious deaths on record
must be that of a reclusive and obviously
mean undertaker named Osbert James
Gardner of Wisconsin, USA who was found
frozen to death in bed, in December 1968.

Mr Gardner, who was 91 and had only
retired from the family morticians business
the previous year, had ordered the heating to

be cut off from his home a few days
beforehand because he considered the fuel
bill exorbitant.

And yet in a coffin which he had had built
years before in preparation for his own death
and which he kept beside his bed was found
. . . over $200,000 in crisp bank notes!

*   *   *

Undertakers have had to accept being the
target of jokes for many generations now.

But in 1977 two irate undertakers in
Brighton really thought the owner of a new
shop sandwiched between their premises had
gone too far when she put up her sign. And so
they promptly lodged a formal appeal against
her planning application.

But were *their* faces red when they learned
what the shop was really going to be used for
– a beauty salon. And the name?

The Body Shop.

*   *   *

A course in 'Death Education' which

consisted of visits to graveyards, mortuaries, embalming parlours, as well as lectures by experts such as priests and undertakers, was organised by Mr James Speaker of Ohio, USA, in the spring of 1978.

Hoping to decrease the natural anxiety felt by many people about what he called this 'taboo subject', Mr Speaker also invented a way of measuring established attitudes towards death – on the FOD (Fear of Death) and DA (Death Anxiety) scales.

'Our aim,' he explained, 'was to modify existing reactions to these natural facts. We used a control group to check our results – which were dramatic.

'All our students became more fearful and more anxious as a result of the course,' he said. 'Those measured on the DA scale were less affected than those on the FOD. But we are making progress. Very soon we shall know how to find a consistent Fear and Anxiety Reversal Programme!'

★　　★　　★

The story of 'Speedy' Atkins and his
undertaker friend, A.Z. Hamock, became
famous all over America in 1980. It happened
after 'Speedy' made his first appearance on
TV – fifty-two years *after* his death!

'Speedy' was a much respected man in his
home town of Paducah, Kentucky, who
tragically fell into the local river and drowned
in 1928. The body was passed into the care of
his friend the undertaker, A.Z. Hamock,
who out of affection decided to embalm
'Speedy' before laying him to rest in the local
cemetery.

By a curious twist of fate, the same river
that had drowned 'Speedy' flooded nine years
later and brought his coffin back to the
surface. In the battered casket, the little man
was found 'looking as good as new' to quote
his wife, Velma.

Because of this, it was decided 'Speedy'
should go on show in the funeral parlour.
And when A.Z. died in 1949, the business
was taken over by Velma Atkins.

Hearing this story in November 1980, the

producers of the nationwide TV show,
'That's Incredible', decided to feature
'Speedy' Atkins.

'When they asked for him to appear on
television, I dressed him up in a tuxedo and
we got right on the jet,' explained Mrs
Atkins.

After making his debut, 'Speedy' became
an overnight star – the talk of America.
Commented one of the show's organisers,
John Caldwell, 'A.Z. did a great job, for
"Speedy" looked like he was still alive – apart
from the fact that his skin was like wood.

'In fact, he was a lot more lively than some
other guests we've had!'

* * *

Story from the *Eastern Daily Press* of March 4
1981:

People are being overcharged on funeral
costs, the Lord Mayor of Norwich, Mr Ralph

* * *

Roe, told the city's health committee yesterday.

'Some people are being taken for a ride by funeral directors,' Mr Roe commented.

* * *

When Mr Charles Schiller of Boston, USA was made redundant by the firm of undertakers he worked for in 1983, he was given what at first sight seemed an unusual parting gift.

But not so, according to Mr Schiller.

'My leaving present of two elm coffins, with brass fitments, may seem ironic,' he said, 'but this is not the case. I have always wanted to set up on my own, and this is the ideal opportunity.'

* * *

With the introduction, in 1983, of letters of the alphabet before the numbers on the registration plates of motor vehicles, a London undertaker found the plates on his

hearse became grimly appropriate the
following year.

Previously, his registration had read 111
URN – but in 1984 when he purchased a new
hearse and transferred the old plates, it
became B 111 URN.

*   *   *

A pitched battle was fought during a funeral
in the black township of Soweto in South
Africa, in April 1984, according to a report in
the *Rand Daily Mail*.

The paper said that nine people were
stabbed in the battle which was caused by
rival undertakers clashing. The incident was
later blamed on 'business jealousy'.

*   *   *

'A grave-digger was turned into a public
relations officer overnight by Left-wing
councillors in Liverpool and told to preach
Militant doctrines, it was revealed yesterday'
– from the *Daily Mail*, 6 November 1985.

166

'Dead Right' might be the most apt comment on this report from the *St Albans Observer* of 5 December 1985:

'The mortuary at St Albans City Hospital is an unhealthy place to be, St Albans councillors heard last week.'

*   *   *

The very latest thing in the death business in America is the drive-in funeral parlour, according to a report from *US Today* magazine of January 1986.

The first of these buildings has been opened in Los Angeles (where else?) and a special feature are the see-through plastic coffins which enable relatives to view their decreased without even having to get out of their cars.

*   *   *

There was a shock in store for residents of Morningside in Edinburgh, Scotland, in February 1986, when they awoke one morning to find this sign unfortunately

erected outside the premises of the local undertaker:

'Do not attempt to enter box until your exit is clear.'

★ ★ ★

There have been some singularly appropriate names for undertakers over the years. Take, for example:

DEATH & SONS
of Bildeston, Suffolk

WAKE & PAINE
of Twickenham, Middlesex

Mr BONES
of Glasgow, Scotland

WILL PLANT
of Swansea, Wales

J. POSTHUMUS
of Grand Rapids, Michigan

GOODY P. CREEP
of Salem, Massachusetts

and perhaps the most notable of all:

GROANER DIGGER
of Houston, Texas.

*   *   *

There are few odder funerals on record than
that staged by the Roman poet, Virgil, who
spent almost £50,000 burying a *fly*!

The funeral took place at Virgil's town
house on the Esquiline Hill in Rome, and was
carried out with 'barbaric splendour' to quote
one report. There were also funeral orations
read by other famous poets, before the fly was
laid to rest in Virgil's grounds.

But there was method in the poet's seeming
madness. For a decree had been passed in the
Second Triumvirate that the lands of the rich
could be confiscated to be given as reward to
returning war veterans. The only exemption

was land in which someone near and dear was
buried – and Virgil claimed his immunity on
the basis of his pet fly!

★　　★　　★

Oscar Wilde (1854–1900) delighted in telling
the story of the fellow countryman he saw
watching a funeral in a rural district of
Ireland.

'Is that a funeral?' he enquired of the man.
'Yes, sir, I'm thinking that it is.'
'Is it anybody of distinction,' Wilde added.
'I reckon it is, sir.'
'And who is it that died?'
'The gentleman in the coffin, sir,' came the
rustic's reply.

★　　★　　★

Knowing only too well the old saying, 'You
can't take it with you', wealthy Joaquin
Felinna, of Vila Boim in Portugal, decided to
have the last word on his relatives whom he
suspected would squander his hard-earned
cash.

And so, in May 1942, as he lay on his death-bed, Joaquim mustered all his strength, gathered together his banknotes in a pile, and ceremonially burned them.

The ashes he then put into an urn – along with a note explaining what he had done and just enough cash to pay for his funeral!

*   *   *

The funeral of Anna Bochinsky was going according to plan in the village of Moinesti in Rumania, in the spring of 1959. The coffin, with its lid open as is customary in the country, was just about to be lowered into the ground, when suddenly the 'corpse' sat bolt upright.

The mourners stood rooted to the spot in dumb astonishment as the woman then jumped from her coffin and without a word ran quickly away.

They were even more horrified when Anna ran out of the cemetery, across the road, and was killed by a passing motor car.

There is a story told in Newcastle about an old woman who was standing outside a Bingo hall waiting for it to open, when a funeral procession suddenly went by.

At this, the old lady broke away from the queue, crossed the road to the hearse, and carefully placed a red rose on the coffin.

When she rejoined the queue, there were several kind remarks passed by those standing alongside her.

'My, what a beautiful thing to do,' said one.

'Eee, not many folks would do that these days,' said another.

And a third added, 'That was a lovely thought, hinney.'

'Oh well,' said the woman after a moment's pause, 'it was the least I could do for him – he was a good husband to me.'

*   *   *

A lucky escape turned into a fatal mistake for Arthur McAlisdair, while he was watching a funeral procession in San Diego, California,

in May 1960. For in order to get a better view of the proceedings, he tried to run across the road in front of the hearse and was knocked over.

Though he was not hurt, Arthur was immediately urged by an onlooker to lie still and feign injury so that he could claim compensation.

Unfortunately, as he did so, the driver of the hearse leapt from his vehicle to see that his victim was all right – leaving his handbrake off in his haste – and the big vehicle rolled forward, crushing Arthur to death.

*   *   *

Returning to his home in Latheron after a research trip in the mountains of eastern Scotland, botanist Mr Fergus Wick was confronted by the sight of a coffin being brought out of the house and placed in a hearse.

Horrified that either his wife or daughter had died during his absence, Mr Wick rushed

moment's stunned silence, he was greeted by
hysterical shrieks.

The mourners – who included his wife and
daughter – were convinced that it was *he* who
was dead and lying in the coffin!

It was later explained that a body had been
found floating in a nearby lake and had been
identified by both Mrs Wick and her
daughter – as well as two family friends and
the local dentist – as that of Mr Wick.

After he had inspected the body in the
coffin, Fergus Wick said, 'It doesn't look
anything like me – but I am glad to be alive!'

*　*　*

Printed in the order of service for the funeral
of Mr Daniel Patrick Murphy of Brooklyn,
New York, in February 1971, were the
following words:

'To relieve the monotony of sitting, while
the coffin is removed for transportation to the
cemetery, mourners are asked to rise during
the singing of the chorus, "Fix'd in His
everlasting seat".'

174

Actor and writer, Jeremy Lloyd, revealed in 1973 that he was leaving the most unusual instructions for his funeral.

'I am always very depressed by graveyards,' he told the *Sunday Express* in October of that year. 'So whatever is left in my bank account I want used to buy a hillside with a cave in it and, wearing my velvet jacket, I want to be put sitting on a chair gazing out of the entrance.

'I think there are one or two fairly cheap caves in the Highlands,' he added.

★   ★   ★

After the funeral service for a close friend in January 1978, two men in Thonburi, Thailand began to argue about the mysteries of life and death. When they then started to dispute the problem of the chicken and the egg and which came first, the argument turned to blows and one man tragically killed the other.

The dead man had maintained it was the egg.

After conducting a funeral service for a well-known local drunkard, Arthur Mage, in December 1978, the Revd James Owen of Cambridge received a number of complaints from parishioners.

'One is never surprised at the lack of charity that exists,' he said of the service which was attended by members of the police force, the local Publicans' Association and Alcoholics Anonymous.

A memorial address was also given by Dr Michael Avon who said, 'Arthur was born to suffer. Often he was mugged for the money it had taken him days to beg.

'It is true that he was a homeless alcoholic who made well over a hundred appearances before the bench,' added Dr Avon. 'However, he once gave me the most perfect definition of the Christian life – unfortunately it was some years ago and I have lost the piece of paper on which I jotted it down.'

* * *

There was a surprise in store for Mrs

Christine Jay when she arrived for a funeral at Studland near Swanage in Dorset, in June 1979. For she had travelled all the way from her home in Montreal, Canada with her husband, for the funeral of her grandmother – only to find the old lady was still alive.

'We were quite surprised to find Granny Dade up and about,' said Mrs Jay.

The old lady herself explained what had happened.

'Most people only meet at funerals nowadays,' said Granny Dade. 'Therefore I decided to have my "end-of-term" party while I was still active. In the end so many people turned up we had to hire the village hall!'

* * *

On the morning of 28 July 1980, a number of family relatives gathered in the home of Mrs Joan Carson of Lake Kushaugua in New York State. They had come to pay their last respects to the lady who had been certified dead from heart disease.

177

As they gazed at the open coffin, however, Mrs Carson suddenly sat up and gazed wonderingly about her.

And at this, her daughter dropped dead from fright.

*   *   *

The bad luck associated with the number thirteen came true yet again in China, in 1983.

On the morning of Friday 13 May, a group of thirteen people were struck and killed by a number 13 train while crossing a railway track in District 13 of Peking.

They were all members of the same family, too – and on their way to a funeral!

*   *   *

The winning letter in a 'Laugh – I Could Have Died!' competition organised by the *Sunday Mirror*, in October 1985, for readers' most embarrassing moments was this entry from Mrs R. Stanton of Chester:

178

'Jumping off a train I saw several members of a family about to get on.

"Oh!" I enthused, "A happy family gathering. How lovely."

' "Actually," came the reply, "we're just going to bury my mother." '

* * *

Eccentric farmer, Vasser Rowe, of Clavering in Essex hated funerals – especially slow-moving cortèges. So he demanded a speedy, stylish send-off when his time came, and that was exactly what his life-long friend the local undertaker, Alan Peasgood, gave him in January 1986.

For during the six-mile journey from Clavering to the chapel of rest in Saffron Walden, Mr Peasgood put his foot down in his hearse and at one point reached the far from funereal speed of sixty-seven miles per hour!

'I'm just sorry I didn't make it to seventy,' Mr Peasgood said afterwards. 'But I'm sure Vasser would have approved. He was a great

character and not a man to dawdle. And it *was* seven miles above the speed limit for the winding country roads!'

* * *

The Americans have come up with a bizarre new form of burial, it was announced recently in *The Mortician's Journal*.

The aim is to reduce the body mass without cremation. First, the corpse is cooled by liquid nitrogen to -100 degrees Centigrade which makes all the body tissue rock solid. Then the frozen body is pulverised by an automatic hammer until all the chunks of bone, head, etc. do not exceed half an inch in size.

Lastly, the particles are reduced to 5 per cent of their original weight by 'freeze drying' which takes out all body fluids.

What is left, the *Journal* adds, 'can be stored in an urn for burial or domestic storage'.

* * *

It will be the ultimate funeral – your ashes despatched into space in a tiny gold-coloured capsule that will remain suspended 1,900 miles above the Earth for 63 million years.

For an estimated cost of $3,900 per capsule, The Celestis Group of Florida, USA plans to launch the first such 'last resting place in orbit' in 1987.

Talking about the plans for these 'space mausoleums' in 1985, a spokesman said, 'With this method, the remains will never be disturbed again – it's not like having to put up with a road going through a cemetery.

'Future mourners will be able to send the sacred remains of their loved ones into undisturbed rest in the sterile, eternal and inviolable space with the stars, planets, Moon and Sun as their markers.

'I'm sure it will be seen by many people as an improvement on scattering ashes on their gardens or on a favourite gold course. It destroys the grass, you know,' he added.

*   *   *

In order to prove whether there was life after
death or not, naval officer Ben Wangford, an
agnostic, requested to be buried in Watford
Parish Church with a fig in his hand. If there
should be an afterlife, he said, then the fig
would germinate in the coffin and burst the
tomb.

Several years after his funeral in 1800, the
officer's tomb *did* split open and a healthy fig
tree appeared.

*   *   *

One of the most curious monuments to be
erected in a cemetery can be found in the
little town of Canden, in Maine, USA.

It is a marble statue some 28 feet high
which towers over the tomb of Captain
Hanson Gregory who died in 1847.

The statue was raised on the centenary of
Captain Gregory's birth to commemorate his
great achievement . . . making the hole in the
doughnut!

*   *   *

The story of the travelling coffin is one of the
most unusual cases of burial on record.

In 1899, the famous actor Charles Francis Coghlan was buried in a cemetery at Galveston, Texas very close to the shore. On 8 September 1900 a West Indian hurricane swept the Gulf Coast of America, and a torrential flood deluged the Galveston cemetery, uncovering and carrying out to sea a number of coffins – including that of Charles Coghlan.

When the hurricane subsided and the tragedy in the cemetery was revealed, no one expected to see any of the coffins again.

But fate had other plans in store. For several months later, after evidently being carried by the Gulf Stream for almost 1,500 miles, the coffin was washed ashore at the appropriately named Fortune Bridge on Prince Edward Island in Canada – the very spot where Coghlan had been born seventy years previously!

*   *   *

Matthew Burnett, a grave-digger in Coventry during the first two decades of this century,

was famous for his wit which was in marked contrast to his gloomy appearance.

A much repeated story is told of a mean local businessman who, after Burnett had buried his wife, tried to get him to lower his fee.

For some time the two men haggled, with Burnett quite unwilling to drop his price for a man he knew was well able to afford it. Finally, the grave-digger lost his patience and glaring at the businessman, pointed in the direction of the grave and shouted:

'Either pay me my due – or up she comes!'

It is said the man paid in some haste!

*　　*　　*

Extract from a letter to the *West Sussex County Times* of June 1949:

'I write on behalf of the churchwardens of St Mary's Church to state we think it desirable to make a change in the arrangements for keeping the grass in the cemetery in order, as Mr Brazly is now getting very infirm. We have given him notice to expire at Christmas.'

Perhaps the weirdest case of coincidence on record was that reported in America, in 1969.

Miles Lucas was driving home from New York to his home in New Jersey when his car was suddenly struck by another vehicle. Miles was slammed against the door and fell out on to the road.

His driverless car then continued to weave along the road until it finally crashed through a wall and came to a stop just beyond.

The wall was, in fact, that of a cemetery, and when the uninjured Miles Lucas arrived to inspect the damage to his car he found it had come to rest against a tombstone bearing the name . . . Miles Lucas!

Statisticians believe the odds against something like that happening are 6,250,000-to-one!

*   *   *

'The lonely ghost' made a cemetery at Lariano, in central Italy, something of a tourist attraction in December 1973. In fact, the parish priest, Father Don Mantani,

founded that only a handful of people
attended his services, while hundreds
congregated outside the cemetery to see the
ghost.

According to reports, there was only one
ghost in the cemetery because it had only
been open a month and contained just one
grave – that of Eva Candidi, wife of a local bar
keeper.

Scores of people reported seeing a figure in
black struggling to get out of the tomb after
the cemetery gates were closed at night.

Said cemetery keeper, Alberto Galante,
'Some people come from their homes after
supper and stand outside the cemetery for
hours – sometimes until dawn – hoping to see
the ghost.

'The other night when I passed by on my
bicycle just before midnight, there were
about 1,000 people peering through the
railings. I think the ghost is lonely, and until
her coffin is joined by others her spirit will
seek to escape.'

★ ★ ★

Topless American dancer, Frenchie Renee, claimed a new world record by being buried alive in a coffin for a month in December 1974 – in company with the four rattlesnakes and a boa constrictor she normally used in her act.

Emerging from her tomb, the exotic dancer from San Francisco drank a glass of champagne and said, 'The burial was the only way I could get a vacation!'

* * *

The Society for Perpendicular Interment announced in Melbourne, Australia, in June 1976, a worldwide campaign to have dead people buried upright in cylindrical cardboard coffins.

An official spokesman of the society said in a press statement, 'This is the only way to solve one of our most pressing problems. Horizontal burial just takes up too much room in our overcrowded world.'

* * *

A decomposed human arm complete with a
hand which was found in a cemetery in
Falmouth, Cornwall, in December 1976, had
a message attached to it which read:

    'In case you need a hand . . .'

*   *   *

You can hear voices from the grave in
America – literally.

    In August 1977, a new gimmick in the
burial business was announced in the form of
the talking tombstone. When mourners got
near enough to the grave it automatically
synthesised a message such as:

    'Hi, there! I was Jane Smith. I died in 1976
on 16 June at 12.05 pm. Thanks for coming
to visit me – and have a good day!'

    Explaining how the tombstones worked
through a speaker connected to a concealed
photoelectric cell, a spokesman of the
manufacturers, Creative Tombstones, said:
'With our computerised system people feel
their loved ones are still with them.'

Widow Mrs Beatrice Dingle of Providence,
Rhode Island announced in August 1978 that
she was suing the local Archbishop, Rodney
Towler, because for seventeen years she had
continuously been praying and leaving
flowers at the *wrong* grave.

She explained, 'I thought my husband lay
beside Rear Admiral Cloker. But when Mrs
Cloker died it was revealed that there was in
fact *no* coffin in the spot adjacent to the
Admiral's.

'I have spent thousands of hours on my
knees and almost $2,000 on flowers – all at
the wrong place. It was wasted time and I
blame the Archbishop!'

* * *

The occupant of a local cemetery was
declared the winner of an election in Texas,
in November 1982.

The unhappy loser of the poll was a
Republican politician, J. Everett Ware, who
was defeated in the election for the South

Central Texas District. It was revealed after the count that the winner was Democratic Senator Wilson . . . who had been dead for six weeks!

★ ★ ★

Alexander Richter of Pennsylvania, USA held a unique record in the annals of burial grounds. For every week for sixty years he placed a wreath on his *own* grave!

As a young man in the twenties, Richter travelled a lot, and after an absence of several years, he returned home to find that the body of a man who had been drowned had been mistaken for him and laid to rest in the family plot reserved for him!

★ ★ ★

The Chinese couple had just been married – but as the report in the *Peking Daily* of 6 January 1983 put it, 'Death could not part them.' For the pair were both dead and attended the service in their coffins!

Although everything else about the macabre ceremony in Shandong Province was as usual – a priest, lots of guests, piles of presents and a marriage feast – the honeymoon was a return to the graveyard.

The 'ghost marriage' had been arranged by the bride's influential parents after she had been killed in an accident – to prevent her suffering the dishonour of being a spinster in the afterlife.

A matchmaker had been employed by the parents to find a suitable husband – and he came up with an unmarried young man who had died a few weeks earlier.

For the ceremony, both bodies were exhumed – and then afterwards returned together to the husband's tomb while the guests stood by 'eating sweets and burning money and clothing as offerings to the couple', according to the *Peking Daily*.

*   *   *

To 'celebrate twenty years in business, the

Scunthorpe Municipal Crematorium held an open day in November 1984.

According to reports, three guides took relays of visitors on forty-minute conducted tours against a background of piped music by Richard Clayderman.

Reported one journalist, 'Before the visitors examined the bone crushers and ovens normally heated to 1,000°F, which take seventy-five minutes to burn an average-size corpse, they were given an explanatory leaflet.'

And Mrs Betty Martin, chairman of the council health committee, said, 'People are curious about what happens in a crematorium and we have been able to allay their fears by showing them. Everyone was delighted by what they saw.'

About 2,000 people attended the open day.

★   ★   ★

It was probably the strangest plan ever to come before the Greater London Council,

according to a report in the *Daily Mirror* of 11 November 1984.

Alternative funerals was the idea – or 'memorial celebrations' as they were to be called – in cemeteries reserved for *Women Only!*

* * *

DEATH'S DOOR

This inscription was put on the grave of William Death, a forebear of the author, who died in Wandsworth, London in 1879.

He was not, though, an undertaker, but a . . . stonemason!